THE FAKING OF THE PRESIDENT

With a touch of makeup even you a meth smoking punk on the streets can grow up to be a Political Superstar

The first ever complete Presidential Campaign Play Book as compiled by an actual Beltway Insider

Written & Illustrated by
Doug Goudsward

gOUDZwORLD
PROductions
Press

gOUDZwORLD PROductions Press
Middletown, NJ, USA
goudzworld@aol.com

First Edition published 2015

The Faking of the President/With a touch of make-up even you a meth smoking punk on the streets can grow up to be a plotical superstar.

ISBN-13: 9780692548523
ISBN-10: 0692548521

1. Humor 2. Politics

For

my mother, Marjorie Polen Goudsward
whose wisdom lead the way

"...the election of the President is pretty well guarded. I venture somewhat further, and hesitate not to affirm, that if the manner of it be not perfect, it is at least excellent. It unites in an eminent degree all the advantages, the union of which was to be wished for."

-Alexander Hamilton - Federalist Paper Number 68: (March 17, 1788)

TABLE OF CONTENTS

INTRODUCTION
(The History of the Presidency)

Early man lived in caves. He survived on a diet of roots and bark. He had no real form of income, and was unable to pay taxes. Having no source of revenue, parasitic governments could not exist. *The World was Paradise.*

Then, man invented the wheel, discovered various means of making fire, and devised new and advanced communication techniques. One would have thought that all this innovation would have only improved on Paradise. **Paradise 2.0,** if you will. But, n-o-o-o-o!!!, it didn't! Suddenly all kinds of problems arose concerning patent infringements on all these new inventions, not to mention congestion on the primitive highways, and pollution of the pre-historic environment. It was obvious that something needed to be done to bring order to this chaos. Instead, governments were created.

... AND TO PAY FOR THE ROADS...
I HAVE *INVENTED* TAXES!

PRIMITIVE POLITICIAN
PREDECESSOR OF *TODAY'S* NEANDERTHALS

Early governments were headed by a person called a "King." There were, in fact, some good kings (i.e. Good King Wenceslas), but most kings ruled like tyrants. They had absolute power and wore absurd clothing that they thought made them look really cool. If you criticized their repressive policies or made fun of their clothes, they would often times have you beheaded.

In colonial North America, in the year 1776 AD, some Yankees decided that they had their fill of this rather unfair arrangement and declared themselves independent of the British monarchy. They forcibly evicted their British overlords and after much debate and internal squabbling put together a blueprint for the fledgling government of America called *the Constitution*.

For the very first time in modern history, **We the People** would be allowed to elect our own leader called "the President" (this is not entirely true, but I'll spare you the very painful details on this until we get to the last chapter on the Electoral College). It was now possible for comedians like Bob Hope, Jon Stewart, and Dennis Miller to make jokes about the nation's leader without fear of being decapitated at dawn. In other parts of the world, people heard some of Bob Hope's jokes or watched *The Daily Show* and decided that they preferred a more suppressive form of government.

At first, it was relatively easy to get elected president. All you had to do was be the general in charge of the army that threw out the British or be an original signer of the Constitution or Declaration of Independence. Today, it is not so easy. The British are now one of our few reliable allies, and if you attempt to sign the original Constitution or Declaration of Independence, it is quite possible that a security guard will shove your face into the double reinforced glass case that houses these sacred documents.

Nonetheless, it is still the American Dream that anyone can grow up to be president. Across America, there are literally millions of people with the required skill set to hold the office. So why is it, when I travel across this great country of ours, all I ever hear is people whining and complaining about the lack of choice among candidates and asking me, "Doug, why must I always choose between the lesser of two evils?" Out of nearly 300 hundred million native born American citizens, why do just an incompetent handful of those eligible to run actually pursue the presidency? It is quite simply because the average person doesn't have even the foggiest notion of how to go about launching a successful campaign. My purpose in writing this book (besides, of course to get incredibly rich and secure a lucrative advisor position in your first administration which

will hopefully segue into an even more lucrative lobbying position) is to encourage more of my fellow countrymen to jump on the campaign bandwagon and throw their hats into the ring for the next election. This will create a larger candidate pool and give *We the People* a greater choice. And after all, isn't that what democracy is really all about?

CHAPTER 1
WHO?... ME?... PRESIDENT?

Wanted: Motivated, natural-bornAmerican citizen 35 years of age or older to lead a major world super power. No previous presidential experience required. Successful candidate should be breathing and must look great in front of a TV camera. Don't delay, file your certificate of candidacy today.

Are you a high school senior? A lazy slacker? Unsure of what direction you should head with your rotten, miserable life? Tired of being unmercifully hounded by your well-intentioned parents for what they term to be "lack of ambition?" How would you like the kind of job that offers lots of responsibility, the opportunity to travel, and the chance to meet all kinds of new, interesting, intelligent, high level people?

If you are thinking about joining the Army, *forget about it!* Chances are you would spend four long years cleaning latrines, peeling potatoes, digging fox holes, and possibly even getting shot at. You would definitely be starting at the bottom. But the career opportunity that I'm going to introduce you to will give you the chance to start right off commanding your *very own ARMY*... **and Navy and Air Force** for that matter. (I wouldn't putz with the Coast Guard, but, hey that's your call!). Best of all, you won't have to deal with all of those petty little rules and regulations that dictate how you should wear your hair or what clothes you have to wear. The position to which I am referring is, of course, none other than that of our nation's chief executive, the PRESIDENT OF THE UNITED STATES OF AMERICA!

FEC FORM 2
STATEMENT OF CANDIDACY

1. (a) Name of Candidate (in full)
   (b) Address (number and street) ☐ Check if address changed
   (c) City, State, and ZIP Code
   2. FEC Candidate Identification Number
   3. Is This Statement New (N) OR Amended (A)
   4. Party Affiliation
   5. Office Sought
   6. State & District of Candidate

DESIGNATION OF PRINCIPAL CAMPAIGN COMMITTEE

7. I hereby designate the following named political committee as my Principal Campaign Committee for the _____ election(s). (year of election)
NOTE: This designation should be filed with the appropriate office listed in the instructions.
   (a) Name of Committee (in full)
   (b) Address (number and street)
   (c) City, State, and ZIP Code

DESIGNATION OF OTHER AUTHORIZED COMMITTEES
(Including Joint Fundraising Representatives)

8. I hereby authorize the following named committee, which is NOT my principal campaign committee, to receive and expend funds on behalf of my candidacy.
NOTE: This designation should be filed with the principal campaign committee.
   (a) Name of Committee (in full)
   (b) Address (number and street)
   (c) City, State, and ZIP Code

I certify that I have examined this Statement and to the best of my knowledge and belief it is true, correct and complete.
Signature of Candidate | Date

NOTE: Submission of false, erroneous, or incomplete information may subject the person signing this Statement to penalties of 52 U.S.C. §30109.

FEC FORM 2 (REV. 02/2009)

Don't say it! I know exactly what you are thinking, "There is no way that I, a smart little teenage wise-ass could ever hope to competently manage this great nation of ours. Maybe a tiny little developing nation in Latin America or perhaps even an obscure former Soviet Republic with a long unpronounceable name ending in the suffix 'istan.' But to be in charge of the good ol' USA? No Way!" Well listen, punk, that kind of an attitude will never make you a winner in life. And quite frankly, your ability to perform the job is not even the issue at hand. Do you honestly think that the question of competency was a deterrent to any of the other individuals who have occupied this exalted position over the last two hundred plus years? I should say not. I mean let's review just a few of the resumes of the men who have been elected to the office over the past 50 years or so.

… A wealthy Boston Ivy League womanizing playboy, ... a Texas cattle rancher … a Georgia peanut farmer… a B-Rated movie actor.. a hillbilly, Ivy League womanizing   playboy… a major league baseball team owner … a community organizer???

What possible qualifications do any of the above positions bring to the table? None that I can see, but they have all produced men who have gone on to be the leader of the Free World. Frankly, it is just a matter of time before this list goes on to include a retired Pro Athlete and a Rock 'N Roll Superstar or Rappa.   So certainly a bright, intelligent person like yourself (you are, after all, reading *The Faking of the President*) should be more than capable of handling at least the most basic rudiments of the job after just mere hours in the Oval Office.

I PASSED!... I PASSED!
DREAMS REALLY CAN COME TRUE!!

Truth be said, according to ***Article II section 1 of the U.S. Constitution,*** there are actually ***only three*** **basic qualifications** required for becoming president, and they really don't set the bar very high. (There is no test involved- It is actually much harder to obtain a valid driver's license in most states!).

BASIC REQUIREMENTS FOR BECOMING PRESIDENT OF THE USA

1. **You must be a natural born citizen or a U.S.citizen at the time of the adoption of the U.S. Constitution.**
2. **You must be thirty-five years of age.**
3. **You must have been a resident of the United States for fourteen years.**

HAVE YOU EVER CONSIDERED THAT MAYBE THE *CONSTITUTION* ITSELF IS *UNCONSTITUTIONAL?*

© 2015 gOUDZWORLD PROductions

But, if you have recently served two consecutive terms as president, then you are automatically disqualified from eligibility. (*If* that is the case, you probably meant to pick up my other book, "***The Milking of the Presidency- Tips on maximizing your personal enrichment from having served as president***" with a forward by Bill Clinton).

So don't despair. I bet that you probably already have met most of the basic qualifications of the presidency. Yes, it is probably true that you will face a lot of pressure in this job. You will be held personally responsible for all the nation's ills. You will have enemies, both foreign and domestic, that will want to see you dead.   Worse still, distant cousins you have never even met will want to come visit you, just so that they can brag to their friends that they spent a night in the White House. But, alas, before you make any hasty judgments and decide that you are infinitely better suited to being a lifeguard at Malibu Beach than the leader of the Free World, you should also consider some of the perks of the presidential position. You will be able to set your own hours. At the drop of a hat you will be able to hop on to Air Force One and be flown anywhere you want, all under the pretense of attending important summit meetings vital to the future of the world. You will have your own private band of secret service agents as your personal bodyguards, and boy do these guys know how to party. But most important of all, you will be surrounded by a bunch of ass-kissing, brown nosing staff members who will grovel at your hallowed feet and will ***guarantee that you will win every single time you set foot on a golf course!***

… And if you should really screw up on the job, so what? Although Congress has twice initiated impeachment proceedings, it is has never successfully ousted a president. And even if that did happen, the presidential experience will still look great on your resume and you'll probably pick up a few gazillion bucks on the side, just off the royalties to your memoirs and fees for speaking engagements.

So does all of this sound exciting? If so, keep reading. What follows is the **first ever, comprehensive, step by step guide detailing how even you, a worthless, crystal meth smoking punk on the street** *can grow up to be The PRESIDENT!*

The Transformation

BEFORE

AFTER

CHAPTER 2
GETTING STARTED

Okay, so now you have decided on a goal in life. Big F***ing deal! For every person elected president, the road to the White House is littered with the road kill of dozens of presidential hopefuls. America is a capitalist nation that thrives on winners and eats up losers alive. Forget all those touchy feely New Age quotes that tell you that you are a winner as long as *you try your best.* When it comes to presidential politics, it is infinitely worse to finish second than to never have tried at all. Think Adalai Stevenson. Adalai who?... Exactly my point. And what about Mitt Romney. Here's a guy who had an amazingly successful career as a high powered Private Equity Management Consultant. He made gazillions of dollars and was the epitome of the American Dream. But since running for president, he is now forever known to posterity (if he is even remembered at all) as "that one percenter multi-millionaire dude who lost to Obama." The last thing America wants or needs is another John McCain, Al Gore, or George McGovern. So if you are going to take the big plunge, (and I don't mean off a bridge in an Oldsmobile with an attractive young staffer at your side) and go for it all, then you damn well better be confident in your ability to headline a winning ticket.

What ingredients are needed to be a winner in this game? That's easy:

1) Some hard work
2) A little luck
3) A dash of experience
4) A whole shit load of *Chutzpah!*

I may have this wrong, but I believe that I heard somewhere along the line that *Chutzpah* is an old Yiddish term defined as, *"having the ability to maliciously hack your parents to death and still be cleared of the crime on the grounds that you are an orphan."* A truly exceptional presidential candidate would also successfully collect on his parents' life insurance policy.

Although the Constitution of the United States of America requires a candidate to be at least thirty-five years of age before allowing him/her to run for the office of president, it is really never too early to start preparing for your future career. This is perhaps best seen through the practical example of our nation's very first president, George Washington. While still just a wee urchin, he had the foresight to stay focused on the ultimate prize, a*nd the office to which he aspired hadn't even been invented yet!*

Case Study: Young George Washington and the Cherry Tree

I know you're all familiar with the basic narrative. You learned it in elementary school. But today, my dear reader, you will be among the very first to *learn the honest to God true,* behind the scenes back story.

It was on a day very much like today.   George was rummaging through his father's tool shed and came across an axe.   He decided to test it out. He figured, "What the heck, my father's most prized cherry tree imported from the finest arboreum in all of England would be as good of a place as any to test out the sharpness of this rusty old blade." He proceeded to the orchard and methodically chopped down the tree.

All evidence pointed directly to the rascally young George. He knew that any attempt to mask the truth would have been fruitless.   It would have quickly morphed into a major scandal. Before you know it, some obnoxious journalist salivating at the chance to build up his reputation would have dubbed the scandal with a witty name like "Cherrygate," (which at that time, at least would actually have been kind of original),   and Georgie Boy's presidential aspirations   would have been dashed before they ever even got off the ground.

Well, GW was too smart to let something like that happened. Instead he proudly admitted what he had done. "Sure , I admit it. *I cannot tell a lie.* I cut down that cherry tree. But it was for the welfare of the nation" [the colonies, technically]. Everybody knows that there is a severe cherry surplus. I figured that if I could do something to cut down on the supply, then cherry prices could be maintained at more stable levels." His argument was so persuasive that today, nearly 250 years later, we actually pay farmers to keep their fields idle even though according to a 2012 report from the United Nations Food and Agriculture Organization there are more than 870 million undernourished people in this world.

This story exemplifies **Campaign Principle # 1:** *Control the Story ahead of the Media!* If you know a story is going to break anyway, be the first one to go out there and tell it. This allows you to create the story's ending before it even unfolds. You can then work backwards to the beginning of the story using *Alice in Wonderland* logic.

Please note that George could easily have averted this entire scandal just by having one of his "hatchet men" perform his dirty work and then disavow any knowledge of the heinous act.   But this technique involves more advanced campaigning techniques which we will discuss later in the book.

Keeping the cherry tree story in mind, it should now be more than obvious that it is never too early to begin prepping for the presidency. Even if you are just a toddler (and if you are, I am quite impressed that you are reading my book… or are you just skimming through the pictures?) you need to start taking the right steps right now to launch your future candidacy.

POP QUIZ:

Q: What is the first requirement for becoming president?
A: Must be a *Natural Born Citizen*

*** VERY IMPORTANT- Note to Self: Before doing **anything else**, get hold of **original** birth certificate .

Ideally, both of your parents are U.S. citizens and you were born within the boundaries of one of the states. It is imperative that you were delivered into this world as a ***natural born citizen.*** It seems like this should be so straight forward, but it is not. The Constitution *does not* even define what a natural born citizen is. Was it the intent of the Founding Fathers to allow for a president from Hawaii? It seems unlikely. Quite frankly, I think they would have struggled with the idea of a Californian as president. But today, at a minimum you want to at least be born in one of the fifty states. Puerto Rico or Guam would just open up a whole new can of worms.

Once you get the whole birth certificate thing sorted out, start pressing your parents (if you haven't already done them in with an axe) to start forking up the big bucks to send you to the "right" nursery school. That way you can start associating with the "right" toddlers who will hopefully grow up to be the "right" people. The importance of knowing *low* people in *high* places cannot be over-emphasized. They can use their money, fame, and power to fuel your political ambition, in return , of course, for various, sundry, and miscellaneous favors from your when you finally make it to the top. This is a concept known as "networking" and it is the only way that anything has ever gotten done.

So go ahead, get out there, and start making those valuable connections. Don't let those pre-school years slip idly by. Use them to get on the fast track. Make the rounds during milk and cookie time. Avoid getting on the whiffle ball team with the most dumb jocks; instead team up with the lawyers and industry captains of tomorrow. You may lose a few insignificant ball games, but trust me, as the years pass by, you will come to realize that there really are some things in life more important than success on the whiffle ball diamond. More importantly, unless you are another Ronald Reagan, don't snooze your way through nap time. Use this valuable hour each afternoon to map your political strategy, while the other hot shots of your generation sleep dreamily. Face it, Kiddies, it is a tough world out there. If you haven't laid the proper groundwork by the time you are six or seven, it will be exceedingly difficult to ever catch up. But don't despair, even if that is the case, we still have lots of tricks up our sleeve. Keep on reading!

CHAPTER 3
CHOOSING A PARTY

The great thing about America is that anybody can grow up to be president. At least that is the popular myth. A much safer statement is that anybody can grow up to *RUN* for president. Of the forty-four individuals who have held the office, forty-two have been heterosexual, white Protestant men. (Of the other two, one was a Catholic and the other had just one white parent). And ever since Abraham Lincoln was elected president seven score and fourteen years ago, all Chief Executives have held political beliefs which fell somewhere within the relatively narrow political spectrum of conservative *Republican* to liberal *Democrat*.

Why do I bring any of this up? After all, the purpose of this book is not to make any type of comment on the state of the social climate in America. Nor am I trying to discourage anybody from running. I bring up this entire issue for just one reason: what it tells you about choosing a political party. *So what is my point?* **If the answer is not intuitively obvious, *Idiot*, I seriously question the value of you bothering to read on. It is apparent that the sole function of your cranial cavity is to maintain a separation between your ear drums. With that level of mental capacity you shouldn't expect to get elected to any office higher than say Congressman or Senator at best.** (please forgive the seemingly abusive language, but I figure I can get away with it, because you obviously have already purchased this book- Don't despair, because if you have gotten this far into the book, you have clearly demonstrated that you are more than capable of receiving some type of lucrative political appointment. And besides, if you are really cut out to be a serious presidential candidate you are going to have to get used to people saying things a hell of a lot worse than this!).

Well anyway, I veer off topic. The point I'm trying to communicate to you is that despite the fact there is a seeming myriad of officially recognized/sanctioned political parties in the United States and that we live in a free country where everyone is entitled to hold his/her own political beliefs and values, you cannot possibly hope to win a presidential election unless you just happened to be a **Democrat** or a **Republican**. So forget about attempting an independent run or joining any of those third parties... *the Libertarians, the Greens, the Socialist Party USA, the United States Marijuana Party, the Know Nothings, or even the Bull Moose Party.* I am sure that they all have redeeming features, but they are never going to deliver you to the oval office. The American people are too pragmatic to fall for any of the ultra right or left wing utopian society crap that these alternative parties promise. A true American knows that it is only by obsessively protecting his or her own selfish interests that any good will ever occur in this world.

SO, a logical question you might ask at this point, is which way should I lean, *Democratic* or *Republican?* (at last , a logical question, *perhaps there is hope for you!*). Going back to the early years of our Republic, it was easy. You didn't even need to choose between the two . George Washington was unanimously elected president twice, and he had *NO* political party affiliation. In fact he was totally against *ALL* political parties. Then, from 1801-1829, four of our all-time greats, (all of whom have been inducted into the Presidential Hall of Fame) Jefferson, Madison, Monroe, and John Quincy Adams (affectionately known to his groupies as *J-Quin*) belonged to a party that was literally called ***"the Democratic-Republicans."*** (What do you boys and girls at **FOX NEWS** and **MSNBC** make of that?). So you still didn't have to choose between Democrat or Republican. But that was a long time ago, in a galaxy far, far away. Today the Democrats and Republicans are clearly two distinctively different parties and according to some evolutionary biologists, possibly even distinct species incapable of inter-breeding. Nowadays, if you said publically that you were a Democratic-Republican you would be put on some kind of anti-psychotic medication and the Democrats and Republicans would spending the next eight years bickering over who should have to pay for your prescription.

OK, so now you know that you have to be either a Democrat or Republican. But how do you actually decide which way you should swing? Well, there are any number of logical ways to make the Democrat-Republican decision. Each methodology is just as good as the other. A few of the more common are:

PARTY SELECTION METHODS

A. Join the political party that your father was a member of.
B. Join the political party that is most popular in your home state.
C. Toss a coin.

Strong arguments can made for each method. **Method A**'s strong suit is that it may provide you with connections within the party. (don't forget the concept of networking that I introduced you to in the previous chapter). **Method B** is effective in that it provides you with a strong base of guaranteed constituents (also known as mindless party-line voters). **Method C**, however, is my personal favorite. Somehow, it seems to be almost scientific.

There are, in fact, a number of software packages available on the market which will help navigate you through the messy party selection process based upon your answers to a series of questions tailored to identify your core values and beliefs. I recommend that you don't squander any precious campaign funds on any of these products. Most political analysts agree that all political party selection methods are equally effective. Don't waste time fretting about this decision because the truth is that it really doesn't matter which of the two parties you join. If you really want to be president, you are going to have to sell out your core beliefs anyway. Furthermore, each party alternately falls in and out of fashion. Generally speaking the party which isn't in power today is the one that is most popular with the general public. Even if your party is not riding the wave of popularity right now, chances are it will be back in favor over the course of the political cycle which can last anywhere from four to eight years. In pursuing a goal as lofty as the presidency, I hardly consider that a long time to wait.

   Once you choose a political party, the decision is not necessarily engraved in stone. It is sometimes possible to give your political career a jolt by jumping parties. Ronald Reagan, arguably the *Godfather of Republican Conservatism* actually began life as a *Democrat. Party jumping* should not be taken lightly, however. If you don't handle this move properly your political ambitions could suffer irreparable damage. Even in the filthy, dirty, backstabbing game of politics, nobody likes a traitor. Also, remember that once you play this card, it is basically irreversible. If you continually bounce back and forth between parties it will be interpreted as a sign of indecision. Even though it is essential to be indecisive if you expect to be a good politician, it is somehow not advisable to advertise that trait to the public at large.

① Mouse released from cage
② Startles Elephant
③ Elephant lands on see saw
④ Donkey Launched
⑤ Grabs Rope
⑥ Lever pulled
⑦ SLOT MACHINE SELECTS Party Affiliation

RUBE GOLDBERG *PARTY SELECTION* MACHINE

CHAPTER 4
GOING FOR THE NOMINATION

At this point, you should have tossed a coin, thrown some darts, or utilized some other rational means of choosing a political party (if you haven't, may I suggest that you get off your lazy derriere and re-read the preceding chapter). From this point forward, your sole purpose for existence on this orbiting planetary toxic waste dump known affectionately as *Planet Earth* is to pursue your chosen party's presidential nomination. This is a grueling process which can take in excess of six years of intensive work.

I've been told that one of the best ways to get a point across is to find a way to relate it to sports. Americans have a strange infatuation with the ability to run, jump, or throw a ball, and often find it easier to grasp concepts about business, science, and even sex (i.e. getting to first base, scoring, etc.) if they can somehow relate it to an athletic contest.

YOU WANT *DEMOCRACY?*... Fine...I'M RUNNING FOR *KING* AND IF YOU *WIMPY* LITTLE *PHILOSOPHERS* WANT TO LIVE LONG ENOUGH TO *DREAM* UP ANY OTHER *BRILLIANT* IDEAS, I SUGGEST YOU *VOTE* FOR ME!

DEMOCRACY'S HUMBLE ORIGINS

Over the years, comparisons have frequently been made between the Presidential Elections and the Olympic Games. Serendipitously, both America and the Olympic Games were born of *the Spirit of '76*; the very first Olympics having been held in the summer of '76 (776 BC that is). The Olympics and the concept of Democracy arose in ancient Greece. Today, as we prepare to elect our next president, this ancient heritage remains very much evident, as most of what our politicians have to say is *Greek to me.* Furthermore, and I don't know if it was by coincidence or design, but both the Olympiad and our presidential elections operate on a four year cycle. None the less, there is, in fact, one extremely significant distinction: **The Olympics offer our athletes the opportunity *to do* what most Presidents can only *dream* about: kicking the asses of the Ruskies and other assorted evil doers from around the world in direct head to head physical competition.**

For this reason, I personally feel more comfortable with a sports analogy that is just a bit more American than the Olympics. So, I will instead develop a comparison between the presidential nomination process and America's other great national pastime, the baseball season. As in baseball, there are essentially four parts to the election season. They are:

1. **The PRE-SEASON**- It starts any time after the previous election and continues on up until the primaries. During this stage, you aren't really worried about winning or losing. You are just testing out your stuff to see if your fastball is still there and to determine whether or not you need to develop a change-up, curve, or screwball.

2. **The REGULAR SEASON**- (The Primaries and Caucuses) Consider each state's primary to be the equivalent of one regular season game. You shouldn't so much be concerned about winning or losing individual games, as long as the entire season is a success. You do of course, want to try to jump out to an early lead so you need to give Iowa and New Hampshire more focus than you may think such small states actually rate. Still, don't get too cocky about early victories or be too discouraged by early defeats. As that late, great political pundit Yogi Berra is often quoted as saying, "It ain't over 'till it's over!" (That's what I love most about sports and politics, you can get away with just continuing to recycle those same old, tired, worn out clichés).

3. **The PLAYOFFS**- (The Convention*) The Party finalists come together for one last round of intensive competition. Just like the baseball playoffs, the conventions are an excuse to whoop it up as hundreds of delegates swarm into town to get drunk and raise all kinds of heck. This culminates with them filing into the convention center carrying banners and rooting on their favorite candidate. Finally, when it is all over, one candidate emerges from the wreckage as the Party Champion, the Presidential Nominee. And he advances on to:

4. **The WORLD SERIES**- (The Presidential Election) The champs of each party go at it to determine who will be the next National Superstar, the President of the United States of America!

Home Plate

If you are already the President or the Vice President, it is easy to launch your campaign. Your merely use your current term in office as a sounding board for campaign rhetoric. Try not to let the management of national affairs interfere with your election efforts. (as vice president, that should not be a problem, because it is not like you even have a real job to worry about) I am assuming, however, that most of you readers do not currently hold the title of President or Vice President.

---

*I know, the winner is already predetermined prior to the convention, but just like a one-sided baseball playoff series, the party officials and media try to hype up the sense of drama.

For the rest of you, it is essential that you get your pre-season kicked off in top form. Hire yourself a slick, Madison Avenue Marketing Team, in much the same manner as you would for selling automobiles, soft drinks, or mobile devices. Instead of offering goods or services for sale, you are marketing a much more specialized commodity, a president. Personally, I think that it is just a matter of time before a new financial derivative, *Presidential Futures*, is traded on the Chicago Mercantile Exchange right up there with pork bellies.

You should direct your market research team to discover what is most on the hearts and minds of the American People. You must learn where the average guy on the street (not to be confused with street people who very rarely vote) stands on the issues. Then prepare a campaign platform which regurgitates these same themes back to the voters in such a manner that it appears that you have created a set of ideas that is truly new and innovative. Ideally, you would be able to stick probes into the brains of all registered voters to find out what it is that they want to hear. For the time being, however, this is both impractical and illegal (unless you are the head of the National Security Agency) so for now, you must use that other tool, the much maligned *public opinion poll.*

Which brings us to **Campaign Principle #2   Present yourself as the only answer to the voter's question: "Who is the candidate that cares about *people like me?"* and play to the people's fantasies.**

Once you determine what the people are looking for in a president, you must select your presidential image type, your ***personal Candidate Brand***, if you will. There are essentially three types to choose from. For lack of a better term, I call them Type I, Type II, and Type III (Hey, the Roman Numerals at least add a touch of distinction).

Type I (The regular Kind of Guy President) *The president next door*, the all around good guy down to earth kind of person. Teaches Sunday School, coaches little league etc. The most important litmus test: *"The president you want to sit down and have a beer with"* **test.** The "every man" strategy was first employed by William Henry Harrison. Now it is a staple of the campaign trail. George W. Bush, Gerald Ford are more recent examples of presidents that fit this mold.

Type II (The Father Figure President) *Older and Wiser, the elder statesman/benevolent leader.* Back in the old days, this presidential type would have been a war hero (many of our more modern candidates have figured out that you could get killed doing that-so they tend to avoid military service at all costs). George Washington and Dwight D Eisenhower are the best examples of this presidential arch type.

Type III (The Charmer President). *Handsome, flashy, smooth talking, and witty.* Preferably a bit of a lady's man, *if you know what I mean* (But hopefully most of the extra-marital exploits don't come out until much later in history!) Frequently known just by his initials such as FDR or JFK. Bill Clinton, of course, is a more recent example of the Charmer.

Then there is also ***the Hybrid Superstar Candidate*** who combines elements of each of the three basic image types. During his prime, many contend that Ronald Reagan fit into this category. Candidates of this caliber are few and far between.

At a point about three to six years before the election that you are going to run in, you should begin expressing your "newly formulated" political philosophy to the public. Also just casually mention to reporters that you might consider running for president, if *"the people" call you to service.* (you always want to make it clear, that the office is a huge inconvenience and not something that you would ever voluntarily thrust upon yourself. It is merely a cross that you must bear for the sake of your nation). Even though you are a total unknown, the mere mention that you are a possible candidate will cause your name to burst into the national spotlight as reporters and pundits begin to speculate on the surprise faces that will be appearing in the long awaited New Hampshire Primary and Iowa Caucus.

Once you start to get name recognition, you want to convince voters that you are not just well known, but quite popular as well. Ask a group of close friends if they will vote for you if you run. Hopefully you can convince nine out of ten to say yes. You then have word leaked to the press that in a recent straw poll, ninety percent of those surveyed indicated that they would in fact support you in your presidential bid. You are now a star on the rise.

For the next several years, you must continue to remain uncommitted as to whether or not you will actually seek the presidency (cite reasons such as your family or the desire to give your current position the full attention it deserves, or any other bogus excuse that you can generate that will play well with the public). Find ways to run a ***shadow campaign.*** By that, I mean that you travel around campaigning without actually admitting that you are running. There are various ways to do this. You could have a ghostwriter write a book under your name and then mount a national book tour. You could try to get yourself appointed to head some type of high profile commission or foundation. Ideally, though, you already hold some other elected office such as Senator or Governor. Then you have the luxury of just using the balance of your term in your existing position to travel around the country ***"not"*** campaigning.

Your name will circulate as the buzz spreads in the newspapers, on TV, and most importantly in cyberspace as to whether or not you will actually run. Finally, in the eleventh hour (a mere year before the election will take place) make the informal announcement to the press that you are going to make the formal announcement next week that you will in fact throw your hat into the presidential race... for the good of the party, and the country, and future of the planet. From this moment on, there is no time to lose; you must appear in public multiple times daily.

...AND IF ELECTED, I PROMISE *KIELBASA* IN EVERY POT, AND I`LL MAKE GENERAL KOSIUSZKO DAY A FEDERAL HOLIDAY!

GAINING FAVOR WITH THE PUBLIC OPINION "POLES"

Some commentators lament that the campaign process has devolved into something that is completely insane and has rendered our political system utterly meaningless. *I emphatically disagree!* The presidency is the most challenging position on the face of the planet, and nothing, *absolutely nothing* can adequately prepare you for the job... but there is *ONE* thing that comes close, and that is to spend a grueling three to six years slugging it out in a campaign. If you have what it takes to run and *survive* a successful presidential campaign, then maybe, just maybe , you also have what it takes to actually serve in the office. For this reason, candidates often erroneously approach a campaign as if it is like going to war. But that is a huge mistake. **Campaign principle # 3** *Approach your campaign as if you are directing an elaborate, entertaining stage show* (You need not look any further than Ronald Reagan).

...Which segues nicely into the next chapter on Public Appearances.

CHAPTER 5
PUBLIC APPEARANCES

I know that you are anxious to get started, but hold on just a second. Before you march right out there in public to make a speech, you need to do a little homework. You have to have an understanding of exactly *who* your audience is. Just one little teensie weensie slip up in public could forever alienate an entire bloc of voters. For example, if you are addressing a group of officials from the *Avocado Growers of America* you wouldn't want to say, "I believe that *guacamole dip* is responsible for ninety percent of our country's juvenile delinquency." Actually, this is a rather poor example. If you made that statement to anybody, they would probably question whether or not you were operating with a full bag of tortilla chips. Nonetheless, I think that you can relate to where I am coming from. It is worth taking a few minutes out of your hectic schedule to inquire discreetly of your campaign manager, "Where the hell are we? " That way you can tailor your remarks specifically to the audience at hand, you cans say all kinds of good stuff they have been longing to hear, and you can win over lots and lots of votes.

CLEARLY I *MISHEARD* THE QUESTION....
I *MISREMEMBERED* THE INCIDENT.
... AND I *MISPOKE* MY ANSWER.

Actually, your campaign manager should already have made certain that your speech writers have prepared the appropriate comments. If he hasn't you should fire him on the spot. I might even consider filling the vacancy, at least temporarily, if you can meet my $10,000 per hour fee and are willing to give my loser brother-in-law a high level cabinet position so that my wife quits pestering me to let him become my partner. As a future president, your time is far too valuable to have to think up things to tell the voters. Contrary to popular belief, Presidents have never written their own lines. Even that myth about sincere Honest Abe Lincoln writing the Gettysburg Address on the back of an envelope on the train ride out to Pennsylvania has been discredited as complete fabrication by some highly respected historians (I mean, honestly, can you picture a president sitting on a train addressing envelopes?).

Even though you should never have to write a speech, it doesn't hurt to know a little bit about the ingredients of great oration. You have already completed step one: Identify your audience. So what's next? You need to string together a bunch of meaningless, rhetorical one liners that the audience can applaud during each pause (and there will of course be lots of pauses). If you are dealing with a group of left-wing, dove, bleeding heart liberal Commie bastards (also known as moderate Democrats) a good number of the attendees may be into that whole "no nukes" kind of thing. In that case why not try dropping a line like this: *I will never bring this nation into an all out, full blown, nuclear war which will wipe out all life on earth as we know it, ... as long as there acceptable, slightly less drastic alternatives.*

ACCORDING TO *SOME* HISTORIANS, THIS IS THE *CLOSEST* THAT LINCOLN CAME TO WRITING A GETTYSBURG *ADDRESS.*

If on the other hand you are going to be talking to a group of Neo-Nazi hawkish right wing conservatives (AKA middle of the road Republicans), it is likely that each member of this rather select group is opposed to both gun control and abortion. Why not try out a line like this: *"GUNS DON"T KILL PEOPLE, ABORTIONS DO!"* I realize that I perhaps have a rather vivid imagination, but I could have sworn that I am already hearing the standing ovation for that one. The great thing about that remark is that you never came out and personally said that you are either for or against gun control or abortion, so you haven't really severed any ties that you might have had with the left.

Which brings us **to CAMPAIGN PRINCIPLE #4:**
NEVER EVER SAY *ANYTHING* THAT PINS YOU DOWN TO ONE PARTICULAR POSITION ON ANY ISSUE!!!

In this day and age, everything you say in public (and probably even in private) is being recorded by somebody and sooner or later, every little snippet will be cut up and re-edited by your enemies to prove that your position on every issue is reprehensible. These little snippets will get replayed on TV ads, on Youtube videos and first thing tomorrow morning they will probably even appear on other digital platforms that haven't even been invented yet. So always be on your guard. Watch every single word that comes out of your mouth. If circumstances allow, don't even speak... just wave, smile and move on. *Eyes are more important than ears!*

...YOU'RE ON *CANDIDATE* CAMERA

Even in the most controlled situations, though, sooner or later, you will have to say something in public. Do not by any means feel obligated to keep your speech dry and serious. Americans want their leaders to be able to entertain them (how else could so many clowns ever have been elected to public office). So go ahead, infuse a little bit of humor into every speech you make. Let us return to the example of Lincoln's Gettysburg Address. That speech was loaded with jokes. No, I am not referring to the boring official text that we are forced to memorize in second grade (at least the evil Mrs. Bates made me memorize it three years in a row in second grade), but the actual original routine that the President did live "on location" for his Home Box Office special. He had that crowd in stiches before he even got up to that "Four score and seven years ago" bit.

You may be tempted to try and say something profound that will memorialize you forever. You possibly envision yourself much like Ronald Reagan or John F Kennedy standing defiantly in front of the Berlin Wall, raising your fist and saying, *"Mr. Gorbachev, tear down this wall!"* or *"I AM a jelly donut!"* Actually, I have had some linguistics experts carefully study the famous JFK Berlin speech and it turns out the whole jelly donut thing is really a misconception... Kennedy actually referred to himself as a Boston crème.. yet another clue for your conspiracy theorists!(... and the Walrus is Paul!)

Ever since 1971, when the 26th Amendment lowered the voting age to eighteen, there has been a trend of politicians going out to the college and university campuses of America in an attempt to appeal to the youth vote. It is not unusual for these candidates to hire rock bands or rap stars to perform at their rallies and to try and throw hip lingo into their speeches. One thing to keep in mind before hitting the college circuit is that college students are, politically speaking, anyway, a very hard bunch to pin down. Many of them are young idealists (translation: spoiled, rich, trust fund, liberal arts majors who have never had to do an honest day's work in their miserable, worthless lives and have no concept of how the real world works). The others are only interested in getting that valuable business or engineering degree and selling their souls to Wall Street or designing weapons of mass destruction for corrupt government contractors.

In speaking to college students, it is probably best just to steer clear of political issues altogether and instead focus on the one subject that they are in universal agreement on: *"the virtues of our TWO PARTY system."* **ONE PARTY TONIGHT, and ANOTHER ALL DAY TOMORROW!!!**

PARTY ANIMALS

What do you do when you haven't even the foggiest notion what the make up of your audience is? Not to worry. Just say things that will play well with everybody. Say that you intend to lower taxes, stimulate the economy, balance the budget, increase GDP (whatever that is), and eliminate the trade deficit. Go for their hearts, not for their heads.   If some heckler should put you on the spot and ask you how you intend to accomplish any of this, just say, "My economic advisors are working out the details of my *New Economic Roadmap for America*, even as we speak. Your economic advisers will probably suffers strokes when they learn that you have said this, but hey, if they can't handle the pressure, tell them you will replace them with someone who can (for some reason, people stubbornly refuse to quit the most miserable of jobs when you say that to them).

No matter who you are addressing or what your speech is about, every speech *must* end with the same stock closing phrase signaling to your dozing audience that it is time to wake up and clap enthusiastically because the speech is finally over . Ironically, it was a phrase first deployed by Richard Nixon in his famed **"I am not a crook"** speech while attempting to work damage control during the heat of the Watergate controversy. It makes blatant use of the *"GOD CARD."* Although it was *never* used by Ford or Carter (the most publically religious president in U.S. history) it was resurrected in Ronald Reagan's first nomination acceptance speech and has become mandatory verbiage by all serious candidates ever since. Come on, sports fans, you know the line I'm looking for. It was plagiarized from a classic Irving Berlin tune. Let's sing together: *"May God bless you and may God bless the United States of America!"*

Regardless of your religious affiliation, most voters want reassurance that you are a God fearing person . Although the phrase has become so over used by candidates that it has been rendered virtually meaningless, failure to say it sends out the wrong signals. So please, no matter what your feelings on this topic are, do not buck the trend.

Lately, it has become increasingly important for candidates to appear on late night comedy shows to show off their "human" side and to appeal to younger voters.   The trend had its early history with a young senator Jack Kennedy appearing on Jack Parr's ***Tonight Show***.   Later, Richard Nixon, of all people, appeared on ***Rowan and Martin's Laugh-In*** and delivered the signature phrase, *"Sock it to me."* The ultimate triumph of the human touch was Bill Clinton, belting out some saxophone licks on the Arsenio Hall Show. If there is a scandal brewing around a candidate, the late night circuit is definitely the place to be; it gives the candidate the opportunity to 'fess up to America, while approaching the topic in a totally light hearted manner that is not to be taken seriously.

Your public appearances serve a two-fold purpose. They serve as a forum for you to gain support for your cause. But just as importantly, they are a major way of raising money. In the early months of the campaign, the latter aspect is probably the most vital. You don't want to become too closely associated with any one set of political ideologies too early, because voters are fickle and it is difficult to predict where they will stand come election time. Besides, it is always easier to *buy* popular support once you have built the financial support.

At the heart of the controversy surrounding fund raising has been the emergence of Political Action Committees, commonly referred to as "PAC's." PAC's are a great campaign tool, so be sure to make maximum use of them. You can use them to go negative against your biggest opponents early without specifically linking your own name to the attack. Your opponent may try to take the high ground and avoid going negative, but that tactic is seldom effective. Then when he finally does try to turn the tables on you, you "cry foul" and profess to be the victim.

More recently, in the wake of the notorious Citizens United case, we have seen the emergence of *PAC's on performance enhancing drugs,* better known as **SUPER PAC's**. In a precedent setting decision, the Supreme Court ruled that **Corporations are people too**, and that *buying* elections with unlimited political contributions is just another form of constitutionally protected freedom of speech. Some activists have gotten their shorts all twisted up over this issue, but I don't see what the big deal is. When rock bands first started getting beer distributors to sponsor their concert tours, the initial reaction from many fans and critics was that these groups had "sold out" to commercialism. Today, however, it is just widely accepted that this is the only way to effectively finance these costly musical extravaganzas. I predict that it is only a matter of time before we similarly accept corporate sponsorship of presidential campaigns. Rather than trying to take futile action to prevent the inevitable wave of the future, I think we should just embrace this development as the ultimate triumph of the capitalist system. In a sense, it would just be a way of bringing out into the light the reality of what has been occurring in the darkness all along. Besides, perhaps fewer politicians will feel a need to engage in unscrupulous activities if they are able to make a few million dollars off the sale of T-shirts bearing the vestige of their smiling face on the front and read on the back as follows:

Shotz Lite Brewery
Proudly presents
JOE BINOTZ
Campaign Tour 2016

Baltimore 5/1/16
Glassboro, NJ 5/2/16
New York 5/3/16
Boston 5/4/16
Cleveland??? 5/5/16
Los Angeles 5/7/16

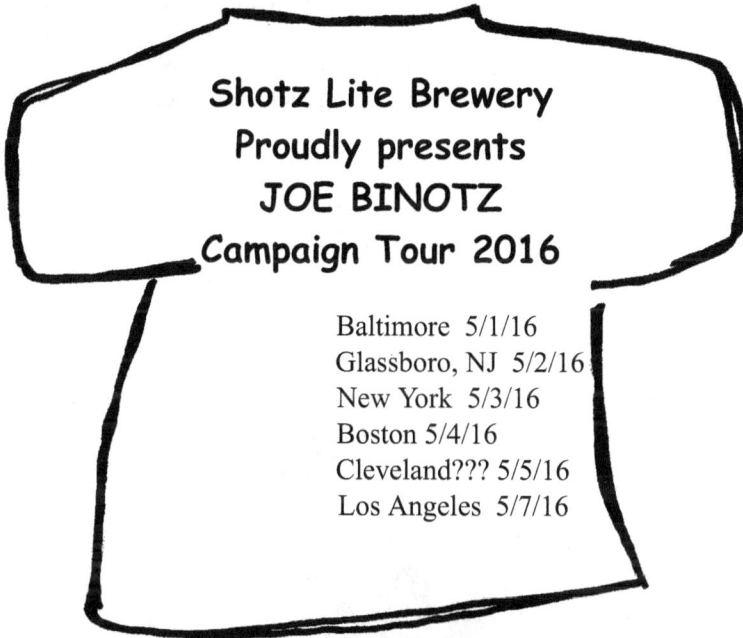

For the time being, however, the best available means of raising cash continues to be the good old fashioned *fund raising dinner.* A successful fund raiser should require a minimum donation of one thousand dollars per plate (to get food on top of it can be extra). I know, your first question is probably, "Who in their right mind would pay one thousand dollars just to go to a fund raising dinner?" Well get this through your thick skull, now that you are a presidential candidate, the last thing in the world that you should be concerned about is people being in their right mind. Besides, when people hear of an exorbitant fee being charged for a dinner, they think that means that only the rich and powerful will be in attendance. To make others think that they too are rich and famous they will happily shell out the big bucks for your lousy catered buffet that should only cost you about ten dollars per head to host. Don't feel guilty though. They deserve it. Besides it takes megabucks to launch even the most unsuccessful of campaigns. There are commercials to be produced, literature to be published and mailed, websites to be designed, salaries and travel expenses to be paid, and of course slush fund coffers to be filled. According to the ***Center for Responsive Politics***, $6 Billion was spent on the 2012 presidential elections. This number is only going to grow. There is no doubt about it, Presidential Campaigning is far and away the nation's biggest growth industry. It is just a matter of time, though, before the Chinese attempt to get their share of this lucrative American Pie for themselves, and let's be honest with ourselves, the Chinese can probably crank out presidents for one quarter of the cost or less.

Now that you have reached the point where you are hosting exclusive fund raising dinners, you can classify yourself as "a serious contender." Things are just starting to get exciting. Keep on reading; the next chapters of this book start getting down to the real nuts and bolts of waging a successful campaigning.

ALWAYS START WITH A JOKE

CHAPTER 6
MASTER OF PRESIDENTIAL SCIENCE CERTITICATION PROGRAM

Unfortunately, even as president, you have to know something. You don't need to know a whole heck of a lot, but you should have at least enough knowledge to be dangerous. You will, of course, have advisors to provide you with most of your required technical information, but you should still be able to babble semi-coherently on a wide range of topics. For this reason, I have put together a self-study certification program designed to equip you with all the tools you will need to be an effective president. Completion of this course of study is certain to give you a competitive edge over all the other candidates. I know that this might seem like a great deal of work (something which I am sure you were hoping to avoid by becoming president), but I cannot over-emphasize the importance of taking the fifteen minutes or so required to review these study guides. It will definitely reap long term dividends. The only prerequisites for this course are the ability to pay the $40,000 tuition fee and the ability to read (I hope this isn't asking too much in an age where 21% of U.S. adults are below a 5th grade reading level, but that certainly doesn't apply to you or you wouldn't have gotten this far through the book).

POLITICAL SCIENCE 100 *POWER POLITICS*

Study time: 2 minutes   2 Credit Units

As president, you will have one major enemy (next to the Media), and that is Congress. Congress resides in a giant duplex called the Capitol. It consists of two houses, the Senate and the House of Representatives. You will find that many members of Congress want your job. The rest just believe that it is their sworn duty as duly elected officials to make your life miserable. They will constantly pass bills that undercut your goals and objectives and usurp your authority. You do have one primary means of recourse, however: "Vito Power" (commonly misspelled "veto"). Just think of Vito as a giant, brainless thug capable of brow beating an unruly Congress into submission. Vito power is not all encompassing, however. If a two thirds majority of both houses gangs up on Vito, he will be overridden, and you'll be forced to go along with whatever those wimps in Congress say.

FOREIGN POLICY 101 *Us Vs Them*

Study Time: 5 Minutes

10 Credit Units

As the future leader of the Free World, you have to have some form of Foreign Policy credentials. That's why you often see governors and congressman who have never stepped foot outside of the USA suddenly taking overseas vacations when they decide to run for President. While at these destinations, they make a point of being seen hob nobbing with those countries' celebrities and political elite, and giving speeches on things they really know nothing about just so they can be perceived as being savvy in international affairs. The truth of the matter though is that when it comes to foreign policy all you really need to know is that there are just two forces at work in this world. GOOD and EVIL. EVIL is determined to dominate the world order and take away such basic human necessities as Rock N Roll, blue jeans, and reality television. They will stop at nothing to achieve this nefarious goal. These regimes are notorious for their blatant disregard for human rights. Torture, suppression of the free press, and confiscation of personal property are daily occurrences for the wretched citizens of these desperate regimes which are inspired by none other than the Devil himself.

The other force at work in the world is GOOD (which in case you haven't figured it out is *US*) Included in this group are, of course, all nations which are our allies. Admittedly, there may be a few bad step children within this group that occasionally display a slight disregard for human rights, and engage in torture, suppression of the free press, and confiscation of personal property in order to get their democratic ideals across. Their hearts are really in the right place, though. If we continue to supply them with sundry military implements, medical supplies, capital investment, and just good old fashion cash, they will eventually come to see the error of their ways and become full blown democracies in good standing.

This course gets double credit because it develops **Campaign Principle #5** *Sell the adolescent view of the world.* Like all issues, foreign policy is multi-faceted and complicated. The average voter does not want to have to grapple with this. Instead just paint a simple black and white world that even a four year old can understand. After all, how else will you ever explain your foreign policy to Congress?

ECONOMICS *1A   VOO DOO ECONOMICS*

Study time: 5 minutes   2 Credit Units

There are numerous economic indicators including the Dow Jones Industrial Average, Gross Domestic Product, and new housing starts to name just a few. But you really only need to be concerned with the two indicators that the general public really cares about:

- a)   Unemployment rate
- b)   Inflation rate

These indices tell how many Americans are working, and if they are working, what their earnings will be able to buy in the way of goods and services. In a Communist nation you don't have to worry about these things. The State controls the hiring of workers and the setting of price levels. In a capitalist nation like America, however, these indices are controlled by the so called, "invisible hands of the free market," (and have you ever tried to box someone with invisible hands?). There are a few steps that you, as president can take to fight high inflation and unemployment. It is pointless, however, for me to discuss them. They generally take many years to have any effect and usually require major sacrifices from the people. It is apparent that these policies will do little or nothing for your political career. Besides, keep in mind the immortal words of the great economist John Maynard Keynes, the Father of Deficit Spending: *"In the long run we are all dead!"*

Instead, you should just reiterate those economic promises that I spelled out in the chapter on Public Appearances. If you do get elected, just change the manner in which economic indicators are measured (For example, the unemployment rate could be adjusted so that it only counts those people who haven't had a job in twenty-five years whose middle name starts with X as being unemployed). Using creative means of measurement, you should be able to manipulate the data so that even if there is a significant downturn in the economy, your campaign promises still appeared to be fulfilled.

QUANTUUM PHYSICS 2^3 *Nuclear Science for the Brain Dead*

Study time: 2 minutes   2 Credit Units

   Periodically, nuclear issues seize the imagination of the public. Novels, movies, and TV shows have all used sensationalist themes focusing on nuclear disaster. Throw in a couple of *minor* real life incidents like Three Mile Island, Chernobyl, and Fukushima, and you suddenly have a very paranoid electorate. For this reason, it is important for even politicians to have a very vague knowledge of Nuclear Physics (unless of course, you are as fortunate as Jimmy Carter was and you have a young daughter who is an authority on nuclear proliferation).

Well, here it goes: All matter is made up of basic building blocks called "atoms." If something is shot at an atom very, very fast, it can cause the atom to split. When an atom splits, it gives off immense amounts of energy. Depending on how this reaction is controlled, the energy released could conceivable zap away all life as we know it. At this point, it should be obvious that atoms are very dangerous things. For this reason, you politicians and children reading at home, should not play with them. Instead, we should leave the nukes in the hands of trained professionals: scientists and generals, who we can trust to watch out for our safely.

FIFTEEN MINUTES AGO I COULDN'T
EVEN SPELL PREZEDUNT... NOW I
Я GONNA BE ONE!

   Well congratulations, you have successfully completed the certification program. I proudly award you an M.S. Degree in Presidential B.S.... Oh, by the way. Did I catch you cheating?... You did? TERRIFIC, in that case you graduated Magnum Cum Laude!!!

CHAPTER 7
DRUGS AND THE PRESIDENCY

OK. If I am going to help you, you are going to have to level with me. We are about to embark on a very sensitive subject, one that you may not really want to get in to with me. *Relax!* I'm not an attorney, but I'm sure that there must be some type of legal arrangement called *"Campaign Manager Privilege"* which means that even under oath, I'm allowed to lie, so as not to divulge any deep dark secrets that you reveal to me.

So, let's get down to it. At some point in your life you have done illegal drugs, haven't you? I don't care if it is has been smoking pot or snorting cocaine, taking a prescription medication that wasn't specifically prescribe to you, or just good old fashioned under age drinking, at some point in your life, you have run afoul of our nation's substance abuse laws. I knew it! Well, there's no need to hang your head down low. You are in excellent company. Over one hundred million Americans have smoked marijuana at some point in their lifetime. Nearly 20% of the alcohol purchased in the United States is consumed by underage drinkers. Countless people, teens and adults, alike have misused prescription or over the counter meds. It is perhaps the greatest irony of the 21st century that, America is engaged in a multi-billion dollar "War on Drugs" while at the same time having a steamy, illicit "love affair" with those very same substances." Needless to say, this is a thorny topic which adds quite a complication to your presidential run.

For our founding fathers, drugs did not even register as an issue. The Constitution does not address drug use. George Washington and Thomas Jefferson both had marijuana fields on their plantations (they preferred to call it hemp), but none of their political rivals ever made an issue about either one of them smoking *rope*. It has been alleged that another Commander-in-Chief, Franklin Pierce, even smoked hashish with the troops during the Mexican-American War, which actually heightened his reputation as a leader with the men.

It is widely believed by historians that the greatest presidential junkie in the history of the oval office was John F. Kennedy. You might say he took the phrase "highest office in the land" quite literally. In fairness, JFK suffered from a wide malady of ailments including a mysterious affliction called Addison's disease, as well as back pain from an injury sustained when the PT boat he commander during WWII was sunk by the Japanese. In order to even function, he required a daily cocktail of drugs that included Codeine, Demerol, Ritalin, Barbituates, and Steroids. So, perhaps the Cuban Missile Crises was really nothing more than a presidential hallucination. In those days, the press was complicit in hiding the truth. They were well aware of Kennedy's medical situation, but all they would ever report on was his back pain... which of course being caused by a "war injury" only enhanced his image as a "hero."

Paradoxically, as the 60's rolled on, and drug use in American Society became rampant, it became less acceptable for a president to engage in drug use. Actually *"unacceptable"* would be the operative word. During the 1988 campaign, Al Gore would gain notoriety as the first modern day presidential candidate ever forced to *"come out"* regarding his drug use. Rumors had begun circulating about Gore smoking pot at Harvard and later while in the Army. These reports became credible enough that poor old *Captain Ozone,* as he has been nicknamed, was forced to address the issue in a news conference. Only one "friend" came forward to talk about what he had witnessed, and he very much down played Gore's drug use. The issue appeared to blow over, but truth be said, because of the haze of pot smoke hanging over him, the 1988 Gore campaign was never really able to gain any traction. That same "friend" would later re-emerge during the 2000 election to announce that he had been coerced by Gore's staff to lie in 1988 and that Al was in fact pretty much your garden variety stoner. This time, around Gore's campaign might have literally, "gone up in smoke" if it wasn't for the fact that his opponent, George W. Bush was also the subject of many credible drug and alcohol fueled rumors.

With Al Gore having already stoked the flames if you will, in 1988, it was now a little easier for Bill Clinton to stand up to tales of his drug use in 1992 . "Yes," he admitted, " I smoked marijuana a few times, ...but didn't inhale." *Wink wink nod nod ha ha!* Over half of America was in on the joke, Clinton was basically given a free pass with that one. Besides, his sexcapades were far more entertaining than any drug use and gave reporters all the fodder they need to keep the presses rolling. But then again, he "didn't have sex with *that* woman" either. But I guess "it all depends on what your definition of 'is' is." Are you confused yet? Bet you're sorry that today was the day that you decide to give up crystal meth or smelling glue.

Even before Barrak Obama decided to run for President, he decided it was probably better to just "out" himself on the whole subject of drug use. (remember Campaign Principle #1 Take charge of the story ahead of the media) In his memoir, *Dreams of My Father*, Obama 'fesses up to boozing, smoking pot, and snorting blow. Although there were a few conservative pundits who expressed shock, that a man who had basically admitted to committing a felony could be a serious candidate for the Oval Office, many conservatives actually decried Obama for overstating his drug use in order to gain some *street cred* and to look cool to younger voters. Once Obama became president, the press was actually more focused on whether or not he was engaged in the *very legal* act of *smoking tobacco* than about his previous illegal drug usage.

We are living at a time where more and more states are approving the use of marijuana for medical purposes (and trust me, just about any purpose can be deemed "medical"). More states are also starting to permit marijuana use for recreational purposes even though it is still a federal crime to distribute it. Is there any clear position that a candidate can take on the drug issue? Navigating this mess is enough to drive any presidential hopeful to drink (or smoke or snort or inject).

So what do you do? The good news for a meth smoking punk like yourself, is that today any good campaign team worth its salt can mitigate any damage that your druggie past may have done to your public persona. The bad news is that it is probably best to refrain from any future drug use, at least until you have served out your term in office. Let us not forget, *High* Crimes and Misdemeanors are still the very grounds for impeachment!

CHAPTER 8
THE CIRCLE OF TRUST
(Friends, Family, & Staffers)

It is a fact of life that we are all judged, or perhaps misjudged, by the company that we keep. Sadly this is particularly true if you happen to be a presidential candidate. While we can choose our friends, when it comes to family members we are simply stuck with the luck of the draw. As a potential president, you can only hope that your beer guzzling brother or ballerina son will shun the media limelight, keep their mouths shut regarding political issues, and refrain from doing anything that might cause you irreparable embarrassment. If they persist at being a focal point of attention, it is probably best just to funnel some secret campaign funds their way, in return for their promise to disappear to some remote island paradise for the next four to eight years.

Campaign Principle #6 *Surround yourself with people who will neither taint you nor out shine you.*

Though you can't pick your family, you can choose many of the other crucial people that will surround you. As distasteful as it may seem, you are going to need to employ surrogates who can do the dirty work for you. They need to plant lies about your opponent and misrepresent his positions. Most importantly, if things go south, they have to be willing to take the fall for you.

One of the most notable positions in your entourage is your vice presidential running mate. Choosing the right person to fit this bill is exceedingly difficult. Finding someone who actually wants the position is harder still. Everyone knows that Vice President is essentially a meaningless position (unless, of course, your name is Dick Cheney, in which case you get to secretly run the country from an undisclosed location). I mean, honestly, what exactly does a VP do. Ask the average guy on the street and you'll get a blank stare. Ask Mr. Vice, himself, and you may get a long winded explanation about being the Speaker of the Senate, and the president's goodwill ambassador, and this and that, but he will tell you very little that really clears up the mystery. The truth of the matter is that other than getting shuttled off to attend the funerals of B and C-level heads of state, the VP is really just kind of sitting around waiting for something to happen to the Prez, so that he can step up and take over.

Regardless of the function, or lack thereof, of the vice president, the fact remains that you must have one. What should you look for in selecting a running mate? Basically, you want someone who will compliment you politically. You want someone who is going to pull in votes that you would not get on your own. If you lean to the left, get yourself a more conservative running mate. If you happened to be from the North East, by all means partner up with someone from the South or Mid West. And if you are gay... for goodness sake, get a straight man into your act!!!

THE WHITE HOUSE ANNOUNCED ITS *NEW* POLICY ON *CHINA* TODAY

Your vice president must be a person that will not contradict you in public. He or she should be someone who hangs out on the sidelines, looks good, and cheers you on (a team mascot, if you will). At all costs, you want to avoid someone with a strong potential of *going rogue*. Run a detailed background check on your prospective running mate before announcing your selection. Make sure that there aren't any skeletons, real or figurative, hanging in their closet. It could be very embarrassing, not to mention politically devastating, if it comes out that your running mate's spouse was involved in some shady real estate deals or wasn't entirely honest in filing his or her tax return. Based on the ill-fated presidencies of Lincoln and Kennedy, it would also appear to be bad luck to select a running mate named "Johnson."

Of far greater consequence than your vice presidential running mate is the person you select to be your First Lady (or First Gentleman as the case may be). First Ladies have always played a prominent role in shaping the history of our nation. The names of these great women just roll of the tongue: Martha Washington, Dolly Madison, Eleanor Roosevelt, Barbara Bush, Hillary Clinton, Michelle Obama, and of course, the unforgettable Mrs. Ulysses S. Grant. Your first lady will be one of your most critical advisors. She will provide you with special insights on everything from the china pattern that should adorn the White House dining room table to which of your other advisors you should shit can. Unfortunately, too many candidates and potential candidates take the First Lady vetting process too lightly, or simply marry long before they develop any presidential aspirations. Hopefully, I have caught you before you have allowed yourself to get trapped into a marriage that will limit your political career to such an extent that you will never get elected to any post higher than Middlesex County dog catcher.

For you high school seniors reading, just remember, before you ask that lovely chica to go to the prom, stop and ask yourself about the kind of First Lady this young thing will grow up to be. If you don't think she can handle the job, just tell her to hit the Turnpike. I can read your mind, you are thinking, "But gee I'm not asking her to marry me, I'm just asking her out on one lousy date!" (and boy is she HOT! Well get over it pal. There's no telling where it could all lead. You just might slip up and fall in love and ruin what once looked like a most promising political career.

In addition to your VP and First Lady, you will also have to pick a Presidential Cabinet… and no, this is not a piece of furniture for the Oval Office where you store the china, but rather a select group of your most trusted advisors. Some of these positions will have to be given to "friends" who did special favors for you over the course of your political career. Other posts should be filled with old college fraternity brothers and drinking pals. Face it, Washington, DC is a hostile city. There will be critics everywhere, so you need to surround yourself with the friendly faces of people that will reassure you of what a really great guy you are, despite all the crap that is written about you in the newspapers and on-line. Still, you should leave a handful of slots open for highly qualified individuals capable of providing you with expert advice.

If you are still with me, then you are doing great. I know that a lot was crammed into this chapter, but next we will lighten things up with a little bit of fashion fun!

CHAPTER 9
DRESS FOR PRESIDENTIAL SUCCESS

You should now have all of the technical knowledge required of a modern day president. Don't think that you are ready for prime time yet though. In this world of video madness, you won't go anywhere if you don't *look the part*. Quite a bit has been written on the topic of what clothing one should wear to succeed in corporate America beginning with John T. Molloy's classic dissertation on the subject titled **Dress for Success** which was first published way back in 1975. Though the styles have been altered somewhat since then, certain enduring principles still stand, and apply to presidential candidates as well. I used to say this book was required reading for all serious candidates. Experience has shown me, however, that most serious candidates can ill afford to waste valuable campaign time educating themselves through reading. I now recommend instead, that you hire one of the overpaid fashion consultants from my firm. Let him or her filter through all of this dry, boring material as well as fuss with the details of actually shopping for your clothing. For the sake of completion though, I will attempt to provide you with the barest fundamentals of presidential fashion, so that you will be able to tell if your consultant is tailoring a wardrobe to suit your needs, or is simply taking you to the proverbial cleaners.

THE PRESIDENT'S NEW CLOTHES

Campaign Principle #7 *Look and act as if you are already president*

If you were to study all the different wardrobes modeled by all the different presidents over the past 225 years or so, you would see an incredibly wide variety of attire. Most notable among the more eccentric get ups includes the shaggy unkempt beard and coarse black top hat sported by Honest Abe Lincoln, and the white powdered wig and outlandish tights favored by General George Washington. You might get the impression that you have open license to wear just about anything that you please. If so, you are sorely mistaken. Put away those tight leather pants and the spiked wrist bands, and change that pink porcupine haircut to something a little more conservative. Remember, even though Abe Lincoln and George Washington might have worn some pretty crazy duds, they never allowed any TV cameramen or aspiring Youtubers to catch them parading around in those costumes. In reality, we don't have any actual photographic evidence that George Washington ever actually even wore those outfits. The only proof that we have are paintings. My own personal conspiracy theory is that these portraits were painted by an artist commissioned by some other political party in a vicious attempt to "swift boat" the Father of Our Country. Then again, so what if he did dress like that. Everybody expected George to be a bit on the crazy side. After all, he had to deal with a problem that no president before or after him has had to face: the prospect of getting termites in his false teeth! (for the uneducated, that is an allusion to the fact that GW was reputed to have a set of rather uncomfortable false choppers made of wood).

Essentially, there are two types of public appearances that you need to prepare for: "Official Appearances" and "Candid Shots." Official appearances are formal events (speeches, debates, ceremonies, etc.). There is only one way to dress for these events, and that is to wear a conservative suit (dark blue or gray), a white shirt (maybe light blue if you are trying to build the reputation of being a liberal) and a tie with a simple power pattern. Be certain to avoid any design that prominently features a crossed hammer and sickle or mushroom cloud. (If you are a woman, you should omit the neck tie). You will be making a lot of formal appearances over the next two years, so you will probably want to stock up with at least a dozen of these Official Appearance outfits.

There is one last detail to attend to though, before your conservative wardrobe is complete: the lapel pin. You and everyone on your staff must accessorize this outfit with the **mandatory** American flag lapel pin. In a case of reality imitating fiction, Richard Nixon's chief of staff picked up on the idea of the lapel pin from Robert Redford's character in the 1972 film, *"The Candidate."* The idea was later resurrected by George W. Bush and his staff in the aftermath of 9/11. Today, failure to proudly display this badge brings your very patriotism into question. Obama tried to buck this trend, but was called out for it by a reporter during a 2007 campaign stop in Iowa. The pin soon reappeared as part of Obama's standard repertoire. Some politicians have tried to customize the pin to suit their individual personalities. I believe, however, that it is safest to just stick with the basic flag design.

The other set of circumstances that you will need to prepare for are the *Candid Shots*. These are pictures and videos which will depicted you relaxing at home with your family, taking a walk along the beach with your spouse and dog (yes, you must have a dog... how bad of a person can an animal lover be?) or eating hamburgers and hot dogs at an old fashion neighborhood barbeque. At these events, you definitely don't want to wear a suit or the American Public will dismiss you as a dweeb. Instead you want to wear clothes that show that you are just another one of the guys/gals (admittedly a regular guy or gal that wants to be in charge of a $3.8 trillion budget and have a finger on the button that could vaporize all life as we know it, but other than that, just a regular guy/gal).

In selecting a wardrobe for these circumstances, you want to wear clothes that are trendy without being flashy or too weird. The biker dude, Goth or gangsta rapper looks are definitely out. Stick to casual attire sold at Macy's, Nordstrom's or some other similar type of store. And please... absolutely positively go for the pre-washed jeans and work shirts. There was nothing more ridiculous than millionaire private equity manager Mitt Romney walking around in brand new perfectly pressed blue jeans that clearly looked like they had just come off the rack pretending that he was just another working class guy.

Don't forget to give some thought to your style of underwear too. No, it is not because you can get away with the baggy pants on the ground look. You just have to be prepared to discuss your choice. During a 1994 appearance on MTV's "Enough is Enough" a young woman asked President Bill Clinton, "Mr. President, the world's dying to know, is it boxers or briefs?" (I personally don't think the world could have cared less). "Usually briefs," Clinton responded and ever since there has been no such thing as *too much information* when a president is out on the campaign trail.

Oh, by the way, during the chapter on Public Appearance, I failed to discuss how you should behave during these informal, unofficial appearances. Please indulge me as I digress a bit and make up for that deficiency now. It is, after all, my book and I can talk about anything I want to. {Editor's note: "Doug, I'll let that line slip through, but if you actually expect to get this worthless piece of shit published, I suggest that you tone down the ego a little."}.

The first thing to note about these informal appearances is that as a presidential candidate, you really don't have the time to spend sitting around the house with your family. You must constantly be out there blazing the campaign trail, pounding the pavement, and pressing the flesh. That is why these so called "candid shots" must really be very carefully staged. Every little detail must be planned out well in advance, from what toys you allow your children to play with (i.e. best not to have them playing with water pistols or G.l. Joe's unless it plays into the anti-gun control or pro-military statements that you will be making) to the way the furniture is arranged, to what magazines "just happened to be sitting" on the coffee table. In general it will probably take your staff three full weeks to properly prepare for the "ad libbed" performances.

Once the campaign gears into full swing, you must be constantly on your guard for hidden cameramen (which in this day and age means anyone who owns a cell phone). They will follow you anywhere just to try and catch you doing something *newsworthy* (translation: improper). Your home will be under constant surveillance. Helicopters or drones will hoover over head. Reporters will be lurking in the bushes. Your bedroom and office are almost certain to be bugged. You won't be safe anywhere.

I might add that this was not always the case. Early presidents could safely engage in scandalous behavior without the press so much as blinking an eye. Thomas Jefferson's plantation was reputed to be crowded with black slaves that just happened to bear a startling resemblance to their famous master. Then there's George Washington. I don't think there is a single structure standing from the colonial era that doesn't boast that "GW slept here." But nobody ever asks, "Oh yeah, with whom?" There weren't painters following him down to a remote Caribbean beach hoping to be able to paint a portrait of Betsy Ross sitting on his lap? But if he was, in fact, such a faithful husband, how did he garner the moniker *"Father of Our Country?"*

Even a hundred years later, nobody really cared very much about a president's sex life. It was a known fact that Grover Cleveland had a bastard son. Opponents used to go to his rallies and chant, "Daddy, daddy!" He nonetheless got voted into office. (Ultimately history got the last laugh as his name is now forever attached to a city in Ohio and a rest stop on the *New Jersey Turnpike*). The point I am trying to make though is that our fascination with our presidents' private lives is a fairly recent phenomena.

During the critical months immediately before the election, you must always be on your best behavior. Every action that you engage in must depict you as a God fearing, family person, with old fashion wholesome values. Your veins must pump red, white, and blue. I realize that this is mainly a matter of common sense, but the following chart provides you with a handful of simple do's and don'ts of candidate behavior. Believe it or not, each election it is inevitable that at least one candidate will engage in something from the **"Don't"** list. To engage in any of the don'ts is certain political suicide. A word of caution: *leave no Chappaquidic Bridges burning behind you.*

DO BE SEEN	DON"T BE SEEN
Playing with your kids and chatting your spouse.	Prancing around with a bevy of scantily clad women outside the Pussy Cat Theatre.
Driving around in a mid-sized American built car.	Driving around in a European or Japanese luxury sedan.
Eating hot dogs, apple pie and vanilla ice cream.	Eating sushi and caviar
Gravely shaking your head while talking to bankrupt farmers in their fields.	Cutting the ribbon to a new factory in China that will put 1,000,000 U.S. workers on the unemployment line.
Attending you God child's baptism.	Participating in a Satanic animal sacrifice.

CHAPTER 10
THE PRESIDENTIAL DEBATES

If you have carefully studied the preceding materials in this playbook , then you are finally ready for the ultimate test, the *Presidential Debate*. This will put to work all of the skills which I have most *humbly* attempted to impart on you over the course of this book. If you are already president, you should attempt to minimize the number of debates you participate in for re-election at all costs. You have absolutely nothing to gain, and everything to lose. You have a very public record as president which is easy to attack. For the rest of you readers, though, a successful performance in the debate can transform your from *dark horse* to *front runner*. I mean who can possible forget the historic Lincoln-Douglas debates of 1858 and the way it brought the rather sticky issue of slavery in a democracy to the center of the American political agenda. I know that I can't but then again maybe it is because every year for three straight years my beloved second grade teacher, Mrs. Bates, covered this famed war of words in excruciatingly painful detail. Despite the great importance attributed to this event by historians and cantankerous elementary school teachers, it was not really considered to be very much of a media event at the time. None of the major television networks covered it, and frankly, I would be hard pressed to name more than one or two cable stations that used it for anything other than filler material. Truth be said, the Lincoln-Douglas debates weren't even a presidential debate; as both men were running for Senate. Nonetheless, it was a watershed moment in the history of presidential politics.

Fast forward one hundred fifty years, and everything has changed. Today tens of millions of viewers tune in across the country so that they can make a rational and informed decision as to who they feel the next leader of the Free World should be. They use a wide variety of criteria ranging from where the candidates stand on certain hot button social issues to where the candidates part their hair. It has become a multi-screen phenomena, as viewers rapid fire millions of tweets throughout the debate sharing their rarely insightful thoughts in real time. Admittedly, many of these viewers are only tuning in because they are participating in a *"Presidential Debate Drinking Game"* whereby they get to chug a beer or do a shot every time one candidate says, "Let me be clear" or perhaps the other resurrects the *"legacy of Ronald Reagan."* But that is a good thing. After enough alcohol, these viewers may actually believe that you are making perfect sense.

As you step out on to the debate stage. remember: you must take charge early. **CAMPAIGN PRINCIPLE #8** *Take charge of the situation and make others play with the cards that you deal.*

Take the offensive. Accuse your opponent of things that he was probably going to try and attack you for. Most candidates try to exploit their opponent's weaknesses. I say attack his strengths. He won't be expecting it, and once you ding the strongest part of his armor, he will easily be defeated. In your opening remarks, tell the world what your opponent's position is, even before he gets a chance to explain it himself. That way, he will be spending the rest of the next two hours trying to clarify what his position really is. If he brings up any hard evidence to support his positions, ignore it. Substitute completely unrelated facts for the truth. If you are really stumped by a question, then just answer it with a joke, and move on to another question.

During the course of the debate, you will be expected to field questions on just about any conceivable subject. For this reason, it is imperative that you keep abreast of current information. I'm told that the *New York Times* and *Washington Post* newspapers are an outstanding source of current event information. Supposedly they are used by intelligence organizations throughout the world to gain valuable insights into events in America. Unfortunately, these publications have a general tendency to stick to dull, dry facts. For this reason I recommend that you instead read the *National Inquirer, Heavy Metal Magazine, People, and Smear Magazine*. Don't limit yourself to print. Today you need to be familiar with the whole gambit of media. Tune in to the Daily Show,   those crazy pundits on the Sunday morning talk shows, and reality TV. Read *The Onion*, and as many ranting weblogs as possible, and of course, tune in your satellite radio to Howard Stern. These sources provide something other than facts; they will supply you with colorful stories and tidbits of gossip which will put you in touch with the real pulse of America.

When confronted with a question during the debate, simply bring some of these human interest stories and anecdotes into play and you will be able to capture the imagination of the American public. Turn everything into a moral or emotional issue.

GENTLEMEN, YOU *KNOW THE RULES.* IF ANY QUESTION MAKES YOU *UNCOMFORTABLE,* FEEL FREE TO ANSWER A *COMPLETELY DIFFERENT QUESTION!*

Below I have provided you with a few simple examples:

Q. Do you feel that welfare reform is necessary in this country?

A. Well let me say this; Just yesterday I learned about a woman in Camden, NJ who was caught trying to mail a pizza with food stamps.

Q. Do you feel that there is fat that can be trimmed from federal agencies.

A. You're darn right. A report came across my desk just last week showing that the Food and Drug Administration literally wasted millions of dollars studying whether or not consumers risked cutting their tongues on wedges of *sharp* cheddar cheese.

Q. What do you think the U.S. should do regarding Iran's nuclear program?

A. Getting back to the subject of consumer finance, let me just tell you a little story about a man on Long Island. He had six demons removed from his soul. But when he couldn't pay the exorcist, he was repossessed.

In addition to keeping up on to date on current events, there are three other points to keep in the back of your head during the debate:

A. ***Don't panic***. If you don't know the answer to question, just answer a completely different question that you have already rehearsed the answer to.

B. ***Use lots of statistics.*** For some reason, people are always impressed with statistics. Again, if you don't know any, just make them up. Yes, reporters will fact check them later, but it is your staff's job to manipulate your answer after the fact so that somehow there will be a kernel of truth to whatever you said.

C. ***Be cordial.*** Always refer to that *scumbag* that you are debating as either "my friend" or "my worthy opponent." Be sure to find fault with everything he says, even if you agree. If you agree with him, then you are de facto endorsing his positions.

After the final statements, your beautiful family should come out and join you on stage. They should give you big hugs and kisses and wear beaming smiles to indicate how proud they are of you. After a few minutes of waving to the crowd, you should all go over to the other side of the stage and shake hands with your opponent and his/her beautiful family. Ideally, *your* beautiful family is *even more* beautiful than *his/her* beautiful family.

Once the actual debate has ended, the real debate begins. Each network and cable station will have an army of political commentators telling the viewers what they just saw (the assumption being that the typical viewer is unable to decipher what just occurred for himself). They will explain which candidate looked best, who seemed to be the most confident, and what each debater "really said." I can't over emphasize the importance of taking these political commentators out to lunch, granting them exclusive interviews, and maybe even discreetly putting them on your payroll. These guys can make or break you. If you screw up, they can cover for you. If you say something really dumb, they can interpret "what you really meant with that phrase." (note: Fox News will of course say that the Republican candidate won the debate, while MSNBC will say that the Democratic Candidate won , so you really don't need to concern yourself with these commentators one way or the other).

The importance of appearance over substance cannot be over-emphasized. It was, in fact, the historic September 26, 1960 debate between Nixon and Kennedy that set in motion the chain of events that has led to the manufacture of today's political candidates. Nixon-Kennedy was the very first true presidential debate and more importantly the first **TELEVISED** presidential debate. It is widely held that the radio audience far and away viewed Richard Nixon, the experienced elder statesman, to be the hands down winner. But hardly anyone really *watched* radio anymore and Vice President Nixon's answers weren't important. Voters *vote with their eyes, not with their ears*. The more youthful and energetic Kennedy, spent the afternoon of the debate working on his tan on the roof of his Chicago hotel while reviewing his notes. He even sneaked in a little nap. When show time came, the rested, confident Kennedy outshined the pale, sickly, sweaty Nixon. For the first time in history, television had decided the outcome of a presidential election.

Seeing what happened to Nixon, Lyndon Johnson refused to debate on television when he ran for re-election. And in his later presidential runs, Nixon had no interest in repeating that mistake again either. Having never been elected, though, Gerald Ford, didn't know any better, so in 1976 he agreed to a series of televised debates with Jimmy Carter. Big mistake... and ever since that day, the presidential debate has been the culmination of the presidential campaign process.

THE DEBATE GOT *HEATED* WHEN THE
TOPIC TURNED TO *GUN CONTROL*

The very instant the debate is over, your press secretary must immediately make the rounds and claim victory, regardless of whether or not the debate was really a win, loss, or draw. ***It is not about winning, it is about appearing to have won.*** You are now on the final sprint to the finish line. All that remains is the *numbers game.*

Chapter 11
THE ELECTORAL COLLEGE (WINNING THE NUMBERS GAME)

So once the debate is over, you must now operate at break neck speed right up until the final closing bell of the polls on Election Day. You, your vice presidential running mate, and your family need to be making constant appearances to boost your profile with the electorate. After all, your ultimate goal is to get the most votes on Election Day, right? Well no... not exactly right. Believe it or not this is not always a game where the *winner takes all.* As a matter of fact there have actually been four incidences where the *popular vote **runner up*** has taken all. Remember when I mentioned *Alice in Wonderland* logic. Well that especially comes into play on Election Day.

Despite everything you may have learned about American democracy, the truth of the matter is that ***"We the People"*** do ***not*** get to vote for president. You say, "But when I look at the ballot, it sure looks like I get to vote for president." When you go into the voting booth, it certainly seems like you are casting a vote for president. But I repeat, the truth of the matter is that American voters do ***not*** get to vote for president. Instead, the voters in each state get to select a small group of people for the **Electoral College** called ***Electors,*** and it is these Electors that vote for president.

The Electoral College *never even actually meets.* Instead, the Electors chosen on Election Day congregate at their respective state capitals on the Monday after the second Wednesday in December. (unless it happens to be a leap year and then...). The selection process for the Electoral College is probably even more confusing and convoluted than the selection process for obtaining admission to an Ivy League College. Each State gets a different amount of electors. The number they get is equal to the number of Congressman that state has in the House of Representatives plus two additional electors, one for each Senator. Obviously, the larger states, with the most Electoral Votes are much more valuable to you than the smaller states.

In most states, *ALL* electors are required to vote for the candidate who won that state's popular vote. In other states, the electors are able to *DIVIDE* their votes between candidates. *But*, nobody is really sure which states are which. It is generally taken for granted that the electors will vote for the candidate that they were supposedly elected to vote for. However, given human nature and Murphy's Law, we all know that someday, perhaps in the not so distant future, the outcome of a Presidential Election will be decided by a *faithless* elector. In that case, the Constitution provides for the president to come from the political party that has gotten to nominate the most standing justices to the U.S. Supreme Court (Well no, it is not specifically written into the Constitution, but if Gore *v.* Bush is any indication, that is how the outcome will be decided).

The Electoral College was the brain child of founding father Alexander Hamilton. He felt that the typical farmer-citizen of his era was too uneducated to make an informed choice as to who should be president. He believed that these citizens should instead cast their misinformed vote for an Elector who would then get to vote for the president on behalf of his state. It was Hamilton's opinion that this system, *while not perfect, was at least excellent.* Today, there are many political experts who feel that this Electoral College mechanism is an outdated anachronism that thwarts true democracy. There are calls for it to be abolished and replaced by a *winner take all* popular vote. It is argued that the Electoral College is inherently unfair. The three most common reasons cited are as follows:

>The Electoral College unfairly favors *large* states
>The Electoral College unfairly favors *small* states
>The Electoral College unfairly favors *medium* sized states

The Electoral College does have it supporters, however and they make one very powerful point that is almost impossible to refute: ***"Hey, didn't we always do it this way?"***

OK. I've just gone through a rather lengthy dissertation on the Electoral College which I am certain has done little or nothing to clarify the issue, so let me cut to the chase, *what does any of this mean to you?* No matter what, Democrat majority states (also called "blue states") are going to award all of their electoral votes to the Democratic Party's candidate. The Republican majority states (called "red states") are going to throw their support to the GOP candidate.

FACE IT... I AM THE *ONLY* CANDIDATE WITH SUFFICIENT KNOWLEDGE OF GEOGRAPHY TO PUT THIS COUNTRY BACK TOGETHER AGAIN.

Don't even waste your time with the Red and Blue States. All you can do is screw up. The only states you should give even the slightest thought about during the final run up to the election are the so called *"Swing States."* Calm down, please! *Swing* does not have any sexual context. These are merely states that do not have a clear cut party orientation, and they hold the key to the final outcome of the election. These states are perhaps, more accurately referred to as battleground states.

WITH JUST FOUR ELECTORAL VOTES TO OFFER, TINY LITTLE RHODE ISLAND IS MERELY A DISTRACTION.

During the final weeks running up to Election Day, you must literally live in these battleground states. Every minute of every day you need to be appearing somewhere. And where you cannot be, you must have boots on the ground representing you. Your people must do nothing short of a full scale military occupation of these states. They must spread the word of your numerous virtues, and even more importantly, encourage those eligible voters most likely to support you to actually *get off of their lazy ass and actually vote.* Ads showing your smiling face must fill the air waves in these states. When those ads are not airing, negative ads taking down your opponent need to be playing.

And as the clock ticks down to Election Day
... one last tip: Don't forget to return to your home voting district to cast that ever important ceremonial vote *for yourself.*

Happy Campaigning and Good Luck!

EPILOGUE
The Last Word

Many historians will argue that the media has always been manipulated by politicians. They will point to such Pre-Revolutionary War evidence as Samuel Adam's staging of the Boston Tea Party and Thomas Paine's penning of *Common Sense* to build their cases. While they can produce some valid arguments, the fact remains that it was not until 1960 that the president truly became a product of the media. The previously discussed Nixon-Kennedy debates of that year forever changed the political landscape. JFK's dynamic visual persona and Nixon's misapplied "Lazy Shave" make-up proved to be poor old Tricky Dick's political undoing (dare I say the first of many?). From that moment on, every action that the president and potential presidents have made has been controlled by the ever present TV camera. We are now at a point where the candidate's make-up artist is probably of greater importance than his running mate. Give him just the right blend of color in his cheeks, dye out the gray, except for just a touch around the temples for distinction, program in the right hand and facial gestures and rhetorical responses, and you are good to go.

Yes, modern technology has certainly come a long way. It can split a seemingly invisible atom to release infinite amounts of energy, it can take a single cell from a laboratory rat, and clone an identical twin, it can create microprocessors small enough to dance on the head of a pin which can execute millions of calculations per nanosecond.   ... And now, we can take an empty human carcass, apply makeup, place it in front of a TV camera, and we can create a political giant, a world leader.

... We can FAKE a PRESIDENT!!!

Repeat after me:

"I do solemnly swear [or affirm] that I will faithfully execute the Office of President of the United States, and will to the best of my ability, preserve, protect and defend the Constitution of the United States."

HAIL TO THE CHIEF

Appendix i: A Day in the Life of a
Presidential Candidate

6:00 AM   Alarm sounds after just having gotten to bed at 4:00AM

6:05 AM   Campaign manager brings in a line of cocaine to get you going.

6:10 AM   Make-up Artist and Fashion Consultant file in to your room to prepare you for your first engagement. While you are being redone, staff members present briefings on the upcoming events of the day. So that the time isn't a total waste, you also wisely thumb through *The Faking of the President* by Doug Goudsward

8:00AM   You look like a million bucks (you should, it cost that much to get you looking that way). Limousine picks you up for your first appearance of the day.

8:30AM   Arrive at a prayer breakfast. Publicly pray for world peace,   solution to world hunger, and a miraculous reunion of the Beatles. (Silently pray that your number one political rival encounters an unfortunate accident or at least a public humiliation)

9:30AM   Address a group of Safety and Security representatives from various federal agencies. Emphasize that you see a strong need for mandatory drug screening, particularly among workers with access to sensitive information or whose jobs impact public safety. Stress the need to rid America of the scourge of illegal drugs.

10:30 AM   Address members of the American Civil Liberties Union. Assure them that your earlier comments were taken out of context. You are against drug screening of any form, and in favor of much more progressive drug laws.

11:00 AM   Hop a shuttle to New York City.

11:45AM   Arrive in New York City. Put on a yarmulke and
            eat lunch in a Jewish delicatessen. (avoid the
            mistake that your rival made of trying to order a
            kosher ham and cheese sandwich). Praise
            the Jewish people for their enduring strength.
            Throw in a few Yiddish proverbs for good
            measure. Emphasize your unconditional support
            for Israel.

1:00PM   Meet with a contingent representing wealthy Arab
          oil sheiks and criticize Israel's aggressive policies
          which are hindering efforts for peace in the
          Middle East.

1:30PM   Board a super-sonic jet to Iowa. While in route
          change into a pair of coveralls and a ball cap that
          says either "Budweiser" or "John Deere"

3:00PM	Jet arrives in Iowa. Take a limo out to a farm that is about to be foreclosed. Drive tractor for a quick lap around a corn field. As you hop back on the jet to head for the Left Coast, tell reporters that you have just gained valuable insights into the plight of America's farmers.
3:30PM	Back on the jet. As the flight heads towards San Francisco change into "street clothes."
4:30PM	Arrive in San Francisco. Take limo out to Golden Gate Park. Spend fifteen minutes sleeping on a park bench, so you can get a taste of what it means to be a homeless street person. Vow to find solutions for the problems of the homeless.
4:45PM	Have Make-up Artist and Fashion Consultant redo you in preparation for you dinner appearance. While this is going on, give permission to a staff member to leak story that your major political rival is a carrier of the ebola virus. (immediately have mini-stroke and forget knowing anything about this.)
6:00 PM	Have dinner with an association of war veterans. Praise these men for their valor and heroism. Emphasize that you too are a former serviceman (do not emphasize that the extent of your military career was doing some light typing at the Military Ocean Terminal in Bayonne, NJ for two weeks during the summer if you actually showed up for your reserve duty at all.)

7:00pm   Hop a shuttle to Los Angeles.

7:30PM   Arrive in L.A. Go to Hollywood and make a special
                guest appearance on the set of a hit television show.

9:00PM   Arrive at an exclusive Hollywood cocktail party.
                Rub elbows with Glittertown's greatest. Make sure
                that your photographer is there and keeps the
                shutter clicking. Maybe even get Jimmy Fallon to
                make a few quips about your golf swing.

1:00AM   Board a jet back to the East Coast

3:55AM   Instruct staffers to come up with some very
                personalized tweets from *you* to the voters, just
                before you go to bed.

6:00AM   Start all over again.

APPENDIX ii

The Official Faking of the President
Online Presidential Candidate Accessories Catalogue

The Ronald Reagan Teflon Vest: Scandals come and go, but *NEVER* stick. Covers all vital organs except the brain (like I said, covers all vital organs). Available in blue pin stripe or desert camouflage.

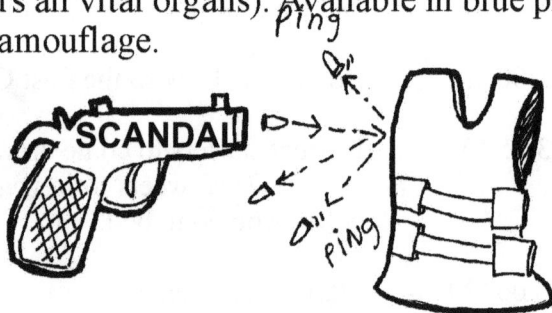

Out Damn Spot, Spot Remover: Patented formula guaranteed to remove stubborn incriminating stains from any intern's blue dress.

American Flag Lapel Pin- The scientifically proven way of showing off your patriotism. A mandatory accessory for any serious candidate, (only available in tri-color *Red, White, and Blue)*

Press Leak Wrench: Is your campaign plagued with leaks? This bad boy is just the ticket. Arm a "plumber" with one of these. When he finds the source of the leak, he just gives it a good healthy bop over the head. Fixes the leak instantly and discourages future leaks from sprouting up.

Presidential Whoopee Cushion: Great fun at Washington cocktail parties. Has practical applications as well. Suppose you are going into a meeting of what is expected to be tough negotiations with a formidable adversary. Simply place the cushion on your adversary's chair before he sits. When he does sit, cushion will make an obnoxiously loud farting sound. He will agree to whatever you say, just to get the meeting over with after that kind of public humiliation. Now available with presidential seal.

ffffssssssshhhhhh

Magic Budget Calculator: A must in these times of soaring deficits. No matter what numbers you crunch in, it always comes up with a balanced budget. Made in China, but designed in America.

***Federal ABDIC (Abbreviation Dictionary*)** An essential reference book in this era of acronyms, New Speak, and AMBGOV (ambiguous governmental terminology).   An absolute must for any serious candidate for POTUS (President of the United States of America)

Presidential Blinders: Fits any size head. Allows you to maintain a narrow view of the world. Also prevents you from seeing what kind of antics your staff may be up to. Helps maximize ***Plausible Deniability*** (the less you know, the better off you are!).

The Richard Nixon Workout: 101 ways to do push ups, pull ups, sit ups, and of course, cover ups. Now available for half price due to the unexplained appearance of an eighteen and a half minute gap on each video.

HALDEMAN... URLICHMAN...
I WANT TO SEE YOU GUYS *JUMP!*

Presidential Flip Flops: The Ultimate in casual candidate foot wear. Each pair contains one flip flop emblazoned on the bottom with "YES" and one with "NO." By merely crossing your legs, you can quickly change your position on any issue.

YES NO

APPENDIX iii

COMMERCIAL SUCCESS (HOW TO MAKE A HIT VIDEO)

Nobody can be a true success these days without first making a hit video. Major sports teams put together music videos before heading into the playoffs or championship games. Videos are used to hype every type of product from candy bars to automobiles. So of course, a video is essential to selling a president.

Just picture this. You are on a set that looks like the main street of a typical American small town. You strut your stuff, talking a rap, while a troupe of perfectly choreographed dancers gyrates behind you. The troupe consist of representative of every major minority, a few token WASP's , and of course some ultra hot young ladies (Though you don't, of course, want to admit it, SEX sells anything, including presidents).

Put together the right video packages, and before you know it, you'll be climbing the charts to the top of the polls. Here are a few sample lyrics you may want in include in your *"Campaign Rap"*

The Campaign Rap

My name is {your name} and I'm here to say,
I think this nation is in disarray.
Now I'm not gonna feed you a log of crap,
I'm just gonna do my Campaign Rap.

I'll balance the budget and furthermore,
I'll find cutting edge ways to feed the poor.
I'll whup terrorism and unemployment too.
And of course I'll lower taxes for you.

I'll make our borders more secure.
And I'll keep us out of a quagmire war.
For every problem, I'll propose a solution,
Even if takes an amendment to the Constitution

I'll get the homeless off the Street,
I'll write a new National Anthem with a funkier beat.
Now at this time you're invited to clap,
'Cause I'm all done with my Campaign Rap.

ELECTION NIGHT FEVER

GETTING DOWN TO THE ISSUES

Appendix iv.
Ten Lies That Presidential Candidates Tell

10.   I never had sex with *that* woman

9.   I will balance the budget *without* raising taxes

8.   I *NEVER* said that.

7.   OK. I said it, *but* remarks are being taken out of context

6.   I *NEVER* did illegal drugs

5.   I am the *ONE* candidate that America can *TRUST*

4.   I would *NEVER* commit American troops to a situation unless U.S. security was at risk.

3.   I believe in increasing *transparency* in government

2.   I didn't know anything about that.

1.   If I had it to do all over again, I would still make *EVERY* one of those decisions..

COULD *HONEST ABE LINCOLN* GET ELECTED TODAY?... SADLY, I THINK NOT...
...THE CONSTITUTION FORBIDS DEAD PEOPLE FROM HOLDING NATIONAL OFFICE.

APPENDIX v.
THE DREADED PRESSURE COOKER PROBLEM

This problem is designed to test your overall presidential savvy and determine if you really have what it takes to be president. There is no right or wrong answer; it is merely geared to get you thinking like a future Commander In Chief. If you are interested, however, in seeing how you stack up against other potential candidates, just jot down your answer, send it to me, care of the publisher, along with a check for $50,000. When the check clears, I'll be more than happy to take five or ten minutes out of my hectic day to critique your handiwork.

THE SCENARIO:

You arrive at the Oval Office at 6:00 AM for what you anticipate will be a routine day. You send a top level cabinet member out to get you a latte and you start to thumb through your In-Basket. There isn't very much in there. A few bills dealing with some boring new trade regulations which require your signature, a message from a high level party official who wants to know if you'll be free for a round of golf this afternoon, and finally a request from the Barksdale, LA Little League Association asking if you will be the keynote speaker at their awards dinner tonight.

A few minutes later, your aide returns with your coffee and a copy of the Wall Street Journal. The Top Headline says that there has been a Stock Market Crash on par with the great crash of 1929.

You decide that you need a little bit of soft background music to mull over what should be done, so you turn on the radio. Instead of soothing music, however, you hear an emergency news flash that there has been a devastating earthquake in California. Everything between Los Angeles and San Francisco that didn't sink into the Pacific Ocean is in ruins.

As you reach to turn off the radio, a member of the Joint Chiefs of Staff (FYI *"joint"* has nothing to do with marijuana) comes running in screaming hysterically about an alarm that has gone off signifying that Russia has just launched a nuclear attack (just when we thought the Cold War was over). After you are able to calm him down, you learn that there have been serious problems with the electronics of the nuclear war alarm system lately, and there is a thirty-five percent possibility that this is a false alarm. If in fact, it is a real attack, the military has just five minutes to respond.

… And then the telephone rings. It is the First Lady. She is crying into the receiver and says that she has to see you right away. If you don't see her right now, she threatens to leave you, which would of course be a major political embarrassment.

Problem: How should you prioritize your schedule for the day? Use the space below which is intentionally left blank for your answer.

Hint: Here are a few partial responses from candidates who have gone on to win election:

1. Call a meeting of your top level advisors and tell them to work out these problems at their level
2. Pray
3. Nuke the Russians until the glow
4. Call that top level party official and tell him that you would love to play golf, just as soon as you iron out a situation with the First Lady, but you'll have to keep it to nine holes because you will be speaking at a Little League Dinner later tonight.

EXTRA CREDIT:
Q. How do you drive a president crazy?
A. Put him in the oval office and tell him that there's a crisis in every corner.
   (you don't get it?... N-e-v-e-r M-i-n-d!!!)

PRESIDENTIAL PURSUIT

HUMBLE BEGINNINGS

START

GO TO "RIGHT" NURSERY SCHOOL COLLECT $5MILLION

CHOP DOWN FATHER'S CHERRY TREE. WIN 5 ELECTORAL VOTES FOR HONESTY

GET INVOLVED WITH THE WRONG PEER GROUP LOSE 25 ELECTORAL VOTES

BECOME A DECORATED WAR HERO. WIN 10 ELECTORAL VOTES

GET ELECTED TO CONGRESS WIN 1 ELECTORAL VOTE

HOLD SUCCESSFUL FUND RAISING DINNER. COLLECT $10 MILLION

REPORTERS TAPE YOU TELLING AN ETHNIC JOKE. LOSE 50 ELECTORAL VOTES

ADDRESS A VETERANS GROUP. WIN 10 ELECTORAL VOTES

BUY A COPY OF "THE FAKING OF THE PRESIDENT." WIN 50 ELECTORAL VOTES'

CHOOSE THE RIGHT RUNNING MATE. WIN 10 ELECTORAL VOTES

PROMISE TO LOWER TAXES. WIN 5 ELECTORAL VOTES

HIGH LEVEL ADVISOR INDICTED. LOSE 15 ELECTORAL VOTES

YOU ARE DOWN IN THE POLLS. PAY $2 MILLION FOR A NEW IMAGE

'OL' CAMPAIGN TRAIL

BEFORE

ELECTORAL COLLEGE

TEXAS

(the Home Game)

DRIVE OFF A BRIDGE. LOSE 100 ELECTORAL VOTES

PHOTOGRAPHER TAKES INCRIMINATING PHOTOS. PAY $40 MILLION HUSH MONEY OR LOSE 100 ELECTORAL VOTES

BEER GUZZLING BROTHER SEIZES THE SPOT LIGHT. LOSE 20 ELECTORAL VOTES

OPPONENT CHEATED ON INCOME TAXES WIN 25 ELECTORAL VOTES

MAKE HIT VIDEO WIN 15 ELECTORAL VOTES

WIN NEW HAMPSHIRE PRIMARY. WIN 50 ELECTORAL VOTES

FEED REPORTERS SOME WITTY ONE-LINERS WIN 10 ELECTORAL VOTES

VACANCY

FINISH

HIRE DOUG GOUDSWARD TO RESCUE FAILING CAMPAIGN. *PAY $100 MILLION*, BUT *WIN 100 ELECTORAL VOTES*

WIN THE FINAL DEBATE WIN 75 ELECTORAL VOTES

YOUR MAKE-UP SMEARS DURING SPEECH. LOSE 10 ELECTORAL VOTES

ABOUT THE AUTHOR (Based On a True Story)

Doug Goudsward was raised in Waldwick, NJ a small, suburban community about twenty miles northwest of Manhattan. At a young age, he seemed destined for Major League Baseball greatness, but alas, he never could quite make the transition from *whiffle ball* in the back yard to *hard ball* on the Little League diamond. His career as a writer almost screeched to a premature halt as well when his second grade teacher, Mrs. Bates, failed to appreciate his homework composition, "I Want To Be a Pimp When I Grow Up" as social satire. The rest of his childhood was relatively uneventful, at least until his senior year of high school when he got his very first taste of political consulting. He volunteered his assistance to Kevin Finnan, candidate for president of the Waldwick High School student council. "Kevin," Doug counseled, as self-appointed campaign manager, "stop wearing those funky checkered pants, get that scientific calculator off of your belt, and by all means, pay the captain of the cheerleaders a few bucks to be seen with you in public. Kevin took the advice and went on to win a dramatic landslide victory in the election. Sources following the election believe that Finnan might have still stood a pretty good chance of winning even if someone had decided to run against him. Finnan himself, denies ever owning checkered paints and a scientific calculator, or for that matter even knowing Doug Goudsward

Not recognizing the potential for great riches in the fledgling field of political consulting, Doug accepted a Navy ROTC scholarship and enrolled at the University of Pennsylvania where he studied accounting and business management (much to the dismay of his parents who used to shrug and say "Why can't he just sit around and play his electric guitar all day like that Springsteen kid?"). Upon graduation, it was off to the Navy where he soon found himself embroiled in *"the big one"* aka Operation Urgent Fury (the U.S. liberation of the medical school on the tiny Caribbean island of Granada with, I might add, minimal disruption to midterm exams). Doug did not see any actual combat action, because *he was off that weekend*. He was, however, engaged in protecting the vital *surfing lanes* off the coast of Long Beach, CA during the immediate aftermath of the hostilities. He would eventually go on to become the youngest Navy Lieutenant ever to be placed in command of an entire fleet (admittedly, it was a fleet of decrepit World War II era railroad cars).

Upon his discharge from the Navy (and yes, it was honorable) he joined a public accounting firm. It soon became evident that he had a great affinity for *figures*. Much to the dismay of the partners at the firm, it was not **numbers**, but *cartoon figures.* With no readily apparent marketable skills, he attempted to earn his fortune in the more traditional fields of investment banking, the New York State Lottery, and Rock and Roll (he professes to have played lead electric tambourine on a track from the Rolling Stones "ground breaking?" (translation: unmemorable) *Bridges to Babylon* album).

Then, in a private moment of desolation, Doug thought back to that magical day in high school when Kevin Finnan rode the tide to victory. Channeling the spirits from that moment of past glory, he had an epiphany that the time had come to make claim on his own destiny. He immediately set about working on an on-line master degree in political science and public policy from the *Electoral College of America.* And now today, in what can only be described as a symbolic fulfillment of his childhood dream, he finds himself embroiled in the BIG LEAGUES playing Hard Ball...*POLITICAL Hard ball!!!*

The author continues to live in a dream world, desperately clinging to the belief that the future proceeds from this book will enable him to sit back and enjoy the life of luxury that he has always deserved.

PLAYING *POLITICAL* HARD BALL

Here is just some of the buzz being generated by
Doug Goudsward and his blockbusting bestseller,
The Faking of the President:

"I didn't read it!"
-Melville Pierre, **The Boston Glob**

"Some of the cartoons were a little bit funny,... I guess."
-Clifton Fadiman, ***The Noo Yawka Magazine***

"Not a book to be put down lightly. It should be hurled with much force."
-Dorothy Parker, **Pundit and professional Know-it-all**

*"That a book like this could be written--published here--sold, presumably
over the counters, leaves one questioning the ethical and moral
standards...there is a place for the exploration of abnormalities that
does not lie in the public domain."*
-**Cirkus Reviews**

*"I'm embarrassed to admit that the author of such rubbish ever made it
through my second grade class, even if it took him three attempts"*
-Mrs. Mary Lou Bates, **Dreaded elementary school teacher**

"Where was Doug Goudward when we needed him in 2012?"
-Anonymous Mitt Romney Staffer (Mitt who?)

"My son, the author...who would have thought!"
-Marjorie Goudsward, **Parent**

*"Phenomenal! Sensational! This book should be mandatory reading for
all serious presidential candidates and students of Political Science."*
-Doug Goudsward, **Famed political author and pundit**

www.ingramcontent.com/pod-product-compliance
Lightning Source LLC
Chambersburg PA
CBHW070552030426
42337CB00016B/2467